TO DIE ON YOUR FEET

TO DIE ON YOUR FEET

—

The Life, Times, and Writings of Práxedis G. Guerrero

—

by WARD S. ALBRO

Texas Christian University Press
Fort Worth

Copyright © 1996, Ward S. Albro

Library of Congress Cataloging-in-Publication Data

To die on your feet : the life, times, and writings of Práxedis G. Guerrero / by Ward S. Albro.
p. Cm.
Includes bibliographical references (p.   ) and index.
ISBN 0-87565-163-1 (hardcover)
1. Guerrero, Práxedis G., 1882-1910. 2. Mexico—History—1867-1910. 3. Anarchism—Mexico—History. 4. Mexicans—United States—Political activity—History. 5. Revolutionists—Mexico—Biography. I. Guerrero, Práxedis G., 1882-1910. Selections. 1996. II Title.
F1233.5.G775A63 1996
972.08'1'092—dc20

[B]
96-20198
CIP

Cover and Text Design by Barbara Mathews Whitehead

CONTENTS

Preface and Acknowledgments / ix

PART I   The Revolutionary

1. The Early Years: Growing Up In Porfirio's Mexico / 1
2. The *Magonistas* Against The Porfiriato / 15
3. On Becoming A Revolutionary / 29
4. "A Notorious Revolutionist"—Until It Killed Him / 47

PART II   The Writer And His Milieu

5. Friends And Foes: The World Of The Mexican In The United States / 71
6. *"Gli Anarchici Nella Rivoluzione Messicana"* / 93
7. "Writing, Writing, Writing" / 113
8. Poet-Revolutionary / 137
9. "To Die on Your Feet": Selected Writings Of Práxedis G. Guerrero / 141

Notes / 169
Bibliography / 185
Index / 191

A Study of the Past Dedicated to the Future

Alex, Ashley, Haley, and Max

PREFACE AND ACKNOWLEDGMENTS

Más vale morir de pie que vivir de rodillas (It is better to die on your feet than to live on your knees). What a heroic statement. My copy of *The Oxford Dictionary of Quotations* attributes it to Dolores Ibarruri, *"La Pasionaria,"* the Spanish republican activist of the civil war era, said to have proclaimed the defiant phrase in a speech in Paris, September 3, 1936. We Mexicanists know that the statement has long been credited to Emiliano Zapata, used to rally his "men of the South." Zapata was killed in ambush in 1919. A 1924 publication in Mexico, however, indicates it was used in print by Práxedis G. Guerrero in his efforts to launch a revolution against Mexican dictator Porfirio Díaz. Guerrero was killed in 1910 in Janos, Chihuahua, in the early days of the Mexican Revolution. He was 28 years old. He died on his feet.

Many years ago, while investigating the development of the Mexican revolutionary movement led by Ricardo Flores Magón, I came to appreciate some of Guerrero's contributions to that movement. My appreciation sustained an interest but did not produce any serious efforts to delve into the life and times of Guerrero until recent years. A return to serious *magonista* studies brought me back to Práxedis. (The proper pronounciation is uncertain. It is either PRAX-edis, with a hard X as in the English pronunciation of MEX-ico, or PRA-he-dis, with the X as in the Spanish pronunciation of ME-hi-co. I opt for the former as Guerrero's friends often referred to him as "Prax," indicating a hard X. I have heard both from people who knew him or knew a great deal about him.)

Because of my interest in the *magonistas*, I initiated and helped organize a *Congreso Internacional: "Homenaje a Ricardo*

Flores Magón" in Oaxaca, Mexico, a few years ago. Dra. Guadalupe Rivera Marín and her Instituto Nacional de Estudios Históricos de la Revolución Mexicana co-sponsored the event with my university, Texas A&M University-Kingsville. We received admirable support from the state government of Oaxaca, the Universidad Autónoma "Benito Juárez" de Oaxaca, and especially from my good friend and colleague, Lucero Topete, director of the Instituto Cultural Oaxaca. I invited scholars from the United States for the event and Dra. Rivera Marín selected the Mexican participants. We soon had a great number of outstanding scholars committed to discussing many aspects of both the man and the movement. When my Mexican colleagues insisted I should be a participant as well as an organizer, I decided that perhaps, even though I had recently published a work on Flores Magón, another topic might add variety to the meeting. I presented a short paper entitled, *"Morir de pie:* Práxedis G. Guerrero and the Mexican Revolution."

That modest effort quickly resulted in more serious study of Guerrero and his writings. I read everything I could find written by him. Because Guerrero—as an expatriate—wrote in the United States, I applied for support for further research from the Recovering the U.S. Hispanic Literary Heritage Project directed by Nicolás Kanellos of Arte Público Press at the University of Houston. The grant helped me bring this work to completion. I am very grateful for this support and particularly wish to acknowledge the encouragement I received from the coordinator of the project, Elsie Herdman-Dodge.

Three friends and fellow historians read this manuscript—a tremendous imposition on friendship—and made suggestions for revisions. John Mason Hart, historian at the University of Houston, knows the period as few others, especially the complexities of the radical movements. Henry C. Schmidt, Texas A&M University historian, is probably the outstanding scholar in this country on modern Mexican intellectual history. Russell Huebel, my colleague at Texas A&M University-Kingsville, brought expertise in United States radicalism and popular culture, as well as a sharp editor's pen to the reading. I also received helpful comments from an anonymous reader for Texas Christian University Press.

I am in awe of translators. What a difficult task! I had a lot of help in translating Guerrero's works. Lydia Méndez, a native of Durango living in Kingsville while her husband studied agriculture, helped me with many of the more "poetic" writings. María de Jesús Ayala Schueneman, a former student now a librarian at the James C. Jernigan Library at Texas A&M University-Kingsville, assisted with many of Guerrero's letters. Jesusita also provided diligent aid in the acquisition of materials through inter-library loan. Another friend and a master teacher of Spanish in Cuernavaca, Mexico, Arturo Ramos, rendered prompt and expert translation assistance. Arturo worked with me on the material in the chapter of selected writings, as well as other writings discussed in the text.

Besides the staff—especially Laura Lucio—at my own university library I wish to thank the people of the other libraries I visited in the research for this book. These include the Bancroft Library at the University of California at Berkeley, the Benson Latin American Collection at the University of Texas at Austin, the libraries at the University of New Mexico and the University of Texas at El Paso, and the San Antonio, Texas, Public Library. I used the extensive resources of the National Archives in Washington, D. C. In Mexico, the staff of the Bibilioteca del Instituto Nacional de Antropología e Historia was helpful. Most of my work in Mexico was done at the Archivo "Genaro Estrada" de Secretaría de Relaciones Exteriores in Mexico City, although I did find valuable sources in the Archivo General de la Nación. I am particularly indebted to Beatriz Carrillo González, an archivist at the Foreign Relations archives, for her assistance in locating materials in both repositories.

I went looking for Guerrero's roots in Guanajuato. Carlos Arturo Navarro Valtierra, director of the Archivo Histórico

Municipal de León, Guanajuato, made the resources of his archive available to me and shared his enthusiastic knowledge and thoughts about Guerrero. A young driver, Martín Jiménez, took me to find the ruins of the Guerrero hacienda, "Los Altos de Ibarra." We took a few wrong turns before we found it was right off the highway between León and San Felipe. At Los Altos, Francisco Longoria, who had spent his life there, as had his father, described life on the hacienda for me.

Collecting photographs led to some interesting, but not always fruitful, searches. I am particularly grateful to Omar Cortés of Ediciones Antorcha in Mexico City for his help. (A native of León, Omar and his brother have an interesting bookshop-cafeteria in that Guanajuato city named *"El Ahuizote."*) Anne Diestal and John W. Roberts of the Bureau of Prisons Archives in Washington, D.C., went out of their way to acquire photos for me. I also wish to thank the staffs of the Arizona Historical Society, the Department of Special Collections at the University Research Library at UCLA, and Nancy Hadley at the Houston Public Library. Carol Tipton, director of the Learning Resource Center, and Gary Longoria, photographic specialist, at the James C. Jernigan Library, Texas A&M University-Kingsville, assisted in several ways.

I have been teaching in South Texas for more years than I like to think about. My university, now named Texas A&M University-Kingsville, does a good job of serving the needs of the South Texas communities. The administrations—and I have seen a few come and go—usually speak of our mission of teaching, research, and service. In the humanities and social sciences, with the heavy teaching loads and numerous other responsibilities, those who research and write do so because they really want to, not because it is supported or even greatly appreciated. I give thanks that my idiosyncrasies have come to be recognized and they let me "do my thing."

A few more thanks. My good friends of long standing, Rosita and Rafael Partida of Cuernavaca, Mexico, provided gracious hospitality while I was doing my research in Mexico City. Judy Alter, director, and Tracy Row, editor, of Texas Christian University Press, are the sort of people who make you want to write books just so you can have the pleasure of dealing with them. My wife, Rosario, gave me a notebook computer for a recent birthday and may have created a monster. As one who could never compose on a typewriter, I was certain the same would be true of computers. I am sure I must have been one of the last holdouts. I thought I would use my beloved "yellow pads" forever. Now I may just write a lot of books.

Ward S. Albro
Kingsville, Texas
Spring, 1996

PART I
THE REVOLUTIONARY

THE EARLY YEARS: GROWING UP IN PORFIRIO'S MEXICO

In 1882 Porfirio Díaz, fifty-two years old, was midway through the presidential term of Manuel González, waiting for a chance to get back into power to continue his mission of bringing order and progress to Mexico. Having come to power in 1876 in what is called the "Revolution of Tuxtepec" under the banner of "effective suffrage, no reelection," Díaz chose to step aside for González in 1880. But his popularity had not diminished and it was only a matter of biding his time until the election of 1884. He passed the years serving in the cabinet of his friend González, serving as governor of his native Oaxaca, and generally basking in the still-favorable reactions to his first term. A year earlier, about a year and a half after the death of his first wife, Díaz married eighteen-year-old Carmen Romero Rubio, a progressive yet pious young woman from an aristocratic family, whose influence and connections would further strengthen Porfirio as he prepared to reassume command. Returning to office in 1884, Díaz would remain there until unseated by the Mexican Revolution in 1911. Toppling the Porfiriato was no easy task, and many died trying.[1] One of the most honored martyrs was Práxedis Guerrero, activist and writer. Born in 1882 in the highlands of Guanajuato, Guerrero, was destined to be one of the principal precursors of the Revolution.

The Revolution, however, could not be predicted in 1882, as Mexicans still optimistically looked to Díaz as the man to bring solutions to political, social, and economic ills that had built up over centuries. Before the revolt of Tuxtepec in 1876, during the first fifty-five years of independent Mexico, the presidency had changed hands about seventy-five times. With governments lasting less than a year on average, it is noteworthy that two, and only two, presidents managed to serve full terms. Mexico had faced serious revolts in the Yucatán and in Texas, wars with France and the United States—the latter ending in the humiliating loss of about half the national territory—and finally suffered the ignominy of the French intervention and the imposition of a European monarchy in the persons of the unfortunate Maximilian and Carlota.

It was in the struggle to rid themselves of the French and the French-imposed regime that the emergence of a sense of Mexican nationalism personified by Benito Juárez became evident. It was in the same effort Porfirio Díaz established himself as a liberal hero. Military skills, heretofore unrealized, brought Díaz to prominence. He was one of the heroes of the Battle of Puebla on May 5, 1862, when Mexico's defeat of the French became so important to the development of a national identity. In the ensuing struggles against the French, Díaz continued to bring glory to himself. A dramatic escape from French captivity added to his stature. With the final withdrawal of French military forces and the capture of Maximilian in 1867, a stern Juárez embarked on a nation-building program with little regard for military heroes.

Díaz returned to his native Oaxaca, accepting land and influence proffered by his grateful countrymen and watched with interest as Juárez laid the groundwork for the establishment of what would become the "Porfiriato." The influence of Comtean positivism in the Mexican education system, with the resulting emphasis on scientific and secular knowledge, order, and progress, gave an authoritarian overtone to Mexican liberalism that had been absent in the presidency of Juárez prior to the intervention of the French. Neither Juárez nor his successor, Sebastián Lerdo de Tejada, hesitated to use the immense power of the executive branch to implement programs that emphasized economic development, railroad construction, education, and overhauling the tax systems. All the reforms were necessary but difficult to accomplish in a nation ravaged by internal and external conflicts for half a century.

Attempted implementation of such programs created enough discontent that Díaz felt strong enough to oppose the reelection of Juárez, and with no success, to raise the standard of revolt under the *Plan de La Noria*, the name of his estate in Oaxaca. After the death of Juárez, Díaz could not prevent the election of Lerdo, but again in 1876, he would revolt under the popular banner of effective suffrage and no reelection. An additional charge leveled against Lerdo in the *Plan de Tuxtepec* was that of selling out the interests of Mexico to the foreigner. In his first term, still consolidating his power, Díaz appeared to work consciously to tie the country to his image as the patriot and savior in a national mission of growth and development. In some respects, these efforts continued during the González interregnum, although many think González maintained an independent position.

Once back in power Díaz governed ostensibly under the

Constitution of 1857, with only minor changes necessary to allow the repeated reelections that maintained a façade of orthodox Juárez liberalism. Díaz conspicuously wrapped himself in the mantle of Juárez liberalism, glossing over the fact that he had revolted twice against Juárez. As noted, Juárez himself had increasingly used a heavy hand to implement his policies. The Díaz regime brought on what some historians style the "modernization" of Mexico. This involved restructuring the Mexican debt to make Mexico attractive to foreign capital; in essence mortgaging Mexico's future in the process. For the moment, however, it worked. In the financial centers of the United States and Europe Mexico was looked on as an attractive and profitable place to invest money.

Tax and land concessions were granted to attract the foreign capital necessary to develop the nation's infrastructure. The expansion of the railroad system provides a prime example: foreign capitalists, with lucrative subsidies from the Mexican government, were primarily responsible for a construction program that gave Mexico 15,000 miles of rail by 1910. This also served to redirect Mexican trade to the north as Mexico and the United States became inseparable trading partners. The north-south development of railroads drew Mexicans from the interior to the borderlands and facilitated the movement of Mexican laborers to various industrial employers in the American Southwest, including railroads and mines.

Mining was also encouraged in Mexico under the Porfiriato. The mining laws of 1884 and 1892 relinquished traditional subsoil rights to promote the development of the nation's extensive mineral resources and, with the aid of foreign investments, increase production of silver, gold, zinc, and especially copper. The rapid spread of the use of electricity was a tremendous boon to the copper industry worldwide; Mexico was one of the prime beneficiaries. Before the Porfiriato was finished, concessions for the development of petroleum resources were granted to United States and British interests. Textile industries were expanded rapidly in Puebla, Veracruz, and Tlaxcala, spurred by investments from French capitalists.

Mexican industrialists also invested in mining and textiles, and the railroads were bought out by Mexican interests before the Revolution. Monterrey, the capital of Nuevo León in the north, began its rise to industrial prominence under Díaz with the development of the first modern brewery in Mexico, the *Cervecería Cuauhtémoc* in the 1890s. In that same city, again with Mexican capital in the lead, the *Fundidora de Fierro y Acero*, the first steel mill in Latin America, began operations in 1900. Little wonder that Díaz was hailed as a hero of the Americas. The rough soldier from the struggles against the French was transformed into a dignified father figure for his nation by his intelligent young wife. Carmen Romero Rubio also served as an intermediary to the leaders of the Catholic Church in Mexico. Although the anticlerical laws of the period of the Reform stayed on the books, enforcement was relaxed. The influence of the Church grew, reflected in greater numbers in the priesthood, and more properties, schools, and religious orders in the country. As the prestige of the Church rose, so did its support for the Porfiriato. As Mexico under the Porfirian system drew closer and closer to the United States economically, Mexicans seemed more and more determined to separate themselves socially and culturally. The upper classes became more Europeanized. In clothes, manners, schools for their children, foreign influences, especially French, prevailed. The architectural styles of Mexico City were copied straight out of Europe.

This erosion of traditional Mexican ways carried over to society in general. Denigration of the indigenous population, and by implication much of the mixed blood, or *mestizo* population, justified economic policies exploiting the lower groups and, unconsciously, laying the groundwork for the Revolution. Only about ten percent of the work force was in industry by 1910, but it was in this area that the exploitation was most obvious and where much of the revolutionary agitation would be directed.

Even skilled workers saw little benefit in the modernization process, as their wages failed to keep up with rising costs. Unskilled workers saw their wages fall twenty-five percent behind the cost of food in the ten or so years before the Revolution. In textile mills, women and children, the most vulnerable and worst paid of all workers, increasingly bore the burden of labor. Attempts to organize workers had little chance of success in the face of opposition from powerful alliances between the factory owners and government functionaries backed by subservient courts of justice.

In rural Mexico the story was even grimmer. By 1910 about sixty-five percent of the work force was still involved in agriculture. The nature of land ownership, however, had changed tremendously by the enforcement of laws from the Reform era on corporate properties and the passage of new land laws under the Porfiriato. Communally held indigenous lands and small peasant land ownership both came under attack. The manner of the enforcement of the land laws, supported by the interpretations of the courts afforded little protection to small rural landholders. Foreigners, as well as Mexicans, acquired huge holdings. The Terrazas empire in Chihuahua, including sons and in-laws, would grow to an incredible fifteen million acres. Between 1883 and 1894 about one-fifth of the land area of Mexico was given over to a handful of companies and individuals. By 1910 little more than 800 large landowners owned more than ninety percent of the rural property. Fewer than ten percent of the indigenous communities in Mexico still held land. The census of 1910 revealed that there were between nine and ten million landless peasants out of a population of about fifteen million. Rural workers in 1910 received less real wages than they had received in 1810. Even some of the hacendados, such as Francisco I. Madero, who would lead the Mexican Revolution in 1910, began to question the costs of modernization under the Porfiriato. But he was not the first hacendado to do so, nor the one to ask the toughest questions.

It was under these conditions that José Práxedis Gilberto Guerrero was born on August 28, 1882, in Los Altos de Ibarra, a hacienda in the state of Guanajuato about forty-five kilometers north-northeast of León. Los Altos de Ibarra is located in rolling, sometimes rugged, mountain and hill country about midway between León and San Felipe, farther to the northeast. The hacienda was in the boundaries of the *municipio* of San Felipe, and it was there that Práxedis was baptized in February 1883.[2] Práxedis was the third from the last of eight children born to the hacendado José de la Luz Guerrero and his wife, Fructuosa Hurtado. The elder Guerrero had acquired his lands in part because of his services to the nearby landed estate of the Jaral de Berrio, one of the most significant holdings in Guanajuato.[3] A namesake uncle, Práxedis Guerrero, had represented a Guanajuato district in the constituent congress which drafted the Constitution of 1857.

Apparently, almost all of Práxedis' first seven years were spent on the hacienda, with seven siblings to minimize the isolation of life in the Guanajuato highlands. Los Altos de Ibarra, as with most such holdings in the Mexican Bajío, was rather self-sufficient, the land supporting corn, wheat, and beans in abundance. Chickens, cows, and horses were the principal livestock and provided the milk, cheese, and meat consumed by the family and the workers. In front of the family home were fruit trees, with peaches and figs produced in large quantities. The main house was large, as might be expected with a family of eight children. Along with the family rooms and bedrooms built around the central courtyard typical of Mexican hacienda architecture, the home contained two kitchens and a small store to sell goods to the workers. Also, in the main house just to the right of the entrance was a chapel where religious services were held, not only for the family but for all the employees and their families.[4]

Although Los Altos de Ibarra was within the jurisdiction of San Felipe, the larger, commercially active city of León provided more economic, social, and educational opportunities.

The family maintained a home there and when he was seven, young Práxedis entered a León elementary school operated by José Lira. He completed his primary education in 1894 in the school of Francisco Hernández. His formal education ended in 1898 after study at the *colegio de* Professor Pedro Hernández, one of the principal secondary schools in León. Guerrero's father acquired his position and substantial economic holdings without university training and did not particularly value study for the "professions," which dominated Mexican universities at the time. No thought was given to Práxedis' attending a university.

The family obviously did foster an atmosphere that encouraged reading, writing, and thinking. An avid reader all his life, Guerrero could draw on a family library that featured the works of Miguel de Cervantes, the French poet Lamartine, Jules Verne, Victor Hugo, Jean-Jacques Rousseau, Camille Flammarión, Pérez Escrich, and the verses of Díaz Mirón. He became fascinated with the writings of Charles Darwin, which possibly weakened the religious beliefs of his childhood. From reading came writing and this, too, Práxedis began early in life. He had little interest in poetry, which is ironic in that later in life and after his death he was frequently described as a "poet." He wrote short stories, and long letters, most often dealing with imaginary events. A sister remembered a very young Práxedis carrying on a correspondence "of ingenuity and wit" with a cousin in which both posed as parents and "Práxedis refused to concede his daughter's hand in marriage to his cousin's son."[5] He published his first work at age seventeen and, with some frequency, submitted articles on general-interest topics to *El Heraldo de Comercio* in León and *El Despertador* in San Felipe.

Despite an early upbringing as a Catholic, Guerrero's intellectual development led him to youthful rebellion against many Church teachings. Some of this doubt led him to sympathetic investigations of Protestantism. Protestantism, he believed, allowed him to learn more of the teachings of Jesus Christ and that, in general, Protestantism "seemed less absurd, and the

Protestants were more sincere and of better sentiments than the Catholics."6 His main contacts with Protestants at the time were with a North American doctor and her husband; perhaps his beliefs were influenced by more than reading. He also read extensively on spiritism and while not ready to adopt either Protestantism or spiritism, his intellectual curiosity gave every alternative a hearing. Ultimately, as his later writings make clear, Guerrero rejected all religion.

Despite his intellectualism, Práxedis grew to maturity at Los Altos de Ibarra with many of the typical interests of a son of a hacendado. Tall for his time (five feet, six or seven inches), handsome, and an elegant dresser, he excelled in such hacienda skills as riding.7 He won numerous horse races in the area. He also participated in bull fights in León as well as the parties and dances with León society that accompanied the *corridas de toros*. A sister remembered him at this time as being energetic and bold, as well as "gentlemanly and loyal with his friendships and commitments," yet still "someone proud and arrogant" with all the foibles common to "young men of his age and class."8 A fun-loving person with many friends of both sexes, he had few close relationships outside his immediate family. The most significant was his friendship with Francisco Manrique from the nearby hacienda Las Fundiciones. Manrique had been a classmate in León and would later accompany Guerrero to the United States, preceding Práxides into revolutionary martyrdom.

In 1900, before his eighteenth birthday, Práxedis and one of his brothers went to San Luis Potosí, apparently in an act of youthful rebellion against parental discipline. They spent several months in that city, supporting themselves by working as laborers in the *Cervecería de San Luis* and later in a smelter. They returned to Guanajauto only after their mother sent family members to persuade them to come home. It was Práxedis' first effort at supporting himself and one of his sisters noted that he returned "more serious and thoughtful and he gave us the impression that his intelligence was clear and subtle."9 It was in

1900 in San Luis Potosí that the beginnings of what would become the opposition *Partido Liberal Mexicano* (*PLM*) could be traced. Some have suggested that Práxedis, who was later to be such a significant *PLM* leader, had his first introduction to opposition politics and radical literature in this rather brief sojourn in San Luis Potosí. This is doubtful. Surely he would have mentioned such experiences in later writings or correspondence.[10]

Some two months after his return to Los Altos de Ibarra, a more mature Práxedis moved to León to handle family mercantile interests. He established a small photo shop there, served as an agent for the life insurance company, *La Mexicana*, and, beginning in July 1901, became the correspondent in León for Filomeno Mata's liberal Mexico City daily, *Diario del Hogar*. His role in the family business also led to numerous commercial trips. Guerrero, accompanying shipments of bricks fabricated at Los Altos de Ibarra and shipped by rail from León, traveled to Puebla, to Mexico City, and to the Texas border town of Laredo. His growing maturity increased his responsibilties on the hacienda, including agricultural production. Horseback travel over the landed estate gave Guerrero a close-up view of rural life in Porfirian Mexico.

At the time General Bernardo Reyes, Díaz' minister of war, was organizing the Second Military Reserve, a citizen militia force. Reyes, oft-times governor of Nuevo León, was seen by many as a possible successor to the aging dictator and the new reserve force appeared to be a potential counter-balance to the federal army. With no apparent concern for the political implications, Práxedis accepted the rank of second lieutenant of cavalry in joining the Second Military Reserve. He learned the art of war from trained instructors and in turn gave military instructions to the workers on the family hacienda and to residents of nearby pueblos, Ocampo and Tlachiquera. Bernardo Reyes, because of actions taken under his direction to suppress the developing Liberal Party movement originating in San Luis

Potosí, was already a villain to the Liberals. The fact that Guerrero joined the reserve is further evidence that his time in San Luis Potosí had not brought contact with any of the revolutionaries-to-be.

In April 1903, still short of his twenty-first birthday, Práxedis found reason to oppose Reyes. That month, Reyes ordered troops to put down a demonstration in favor of a gubernatorial opponent in the Plaza Zaragoza in Monterrey, Nuevo León—action that led to bloodshed.[11] Guerrero resigned his military position in protest, but did not immediately assume an active opposition role. The remainder of the year he continued his work in the family businesses. Early in 1904 his father, José de la Luz Guerrero, became seriously ill, and for the next six months Práxedis was with his father virtually around the clock. His intellectual development continued through reading books by such authors as Maksim Gorky, Leo Tolstoy, Mikhail Bakunin, and Pyotr Kropotkin. Dr. Luis Osollo, a well-known physician from San Felipe, stayed at Los Altos de Ibarra for a time attending the elder Guerrero. Práxedis furthered his education by discussing historic, scientific, and religious questions with the doctor, who would later die in the Revolution serving the cause of Francisco I. Madero.

When his father recovered enough to travel, Práxedis took him to Puebla to take the medicinal baths of *Rancho Colorado*. They stayed there slightly over two months, Práxedis swimming, making solitary excursions to nearby villages and historic sites, and reading—particularly, the works of Jean-Jacques Rousseau. His time alone gave him a great amount of time to think. Visiting the ruins of the forts where Mexican forces achieved everlasting fame by defeating the French on May 5, 1862, Guerrero wrote:

> The cracked, somber skeleton of demolished walls, shows . . . the workings of time that changes everything. Like you, the patriotism of the man who defended you in

62 is a rampart riddled with cracks, a fortified tower converted into rubble where filthy reptiles and bugs live and crawl.

The wind bellows, it blows past your loopholes imitating cries of anguish, terrifying murmurs of corpses that get up and with their hoarse accent sing a bellicose symphony. Sometimes it becomes deafening and seems to distinguish the shout of liberty among the redoubling of the drum and the roll of the artillery. Over there . . . the Fort of Guadalupe on the untilled hill seems to epitomize with its silence the sphinx of the Levitical city. The silence, and the abandonment of those walls makes a world of ideas palpitate in my brain.[12]

Early in August 1904, on returning to Los Altos de Ibarra with his father apparently recovered, Práxedis greeted the hacienda like a lost love:

Many times I have arrived at the old house after having made a painful pilgrimage in the world, but never had it presented before my flattered vision fields so full of sweet memories and brilliant views, so poetic, so loving, offering me the perfume of their flowers and the caress of their breeze, like loving absence offers to our kisses the throbbing carmine crimson of their lips and embraces us tenderly against their heart. . . .
Similar to that indescribable inebriation felt in the squeeze of an embrace of the virgin of our first dreams; that is how I have felt upon letting myself fall drunk of sweet melancholy in the splendid lap of this nature friend. And it seems that soft waves come to me with the echo of a mysterious and distant song. . . . It is the strange melopoeia that the wind makes pass by the green foliage and that seems to say to me: Welcome, oh old friend! Welcome, oh sad pilgrim![13]

Possibly his emotional homecoming from Puebla reflected

the emotions aroused by his decision to leave Mexico. Telling his parents he wanted to go to the United States to study the civilization and culture of the North American people, it seems clear he sought answers to more complex questions. On September 21, 1904, just twenty-two years old, Práxedis wrote, "Tomorrow I will leave, perhaps forever, Mexican soil."[14] He went to León with Francisco Manrique and another friend, Manuel Vázquez, both of whom would join him on the trek north. A postcard dated September 25, 1904, notified his family that he had arrived in El Paso, Texas. He and Manrique went directly to Colorado, where they quickly found employment with a Denver mining concern, The Colorado Supply Company. Breaking the ties with home, especially the closeness with his mother, was not easy for the young Mexican. He wrote in his notebook in December: "Only your memory fills my thoughts, Mother of mine! If I die, the last sigh that escapes my bosom will go to you, the last name that my lips pronounce will be yours, Mother dear!"[15] Fructuosa Hurtado de Guerrero stayed on her son's mind in the ensuing days. In the first days of 1905 Práxedis and Manrique quit their Colorado jobs and set out for San Francisco. Running out of money enroute they worked for a time as lumberjacks, living in a cabin in the woods. On January 11, 1905, Guerrero made these notes in his notebook:

> It rains. . . .
> The openings of the sad and solitary forest allows one to see pieces of brownish sky. .
> Here the river. . . .
> Over there, the silent and scrawny trees. . . .
> Further away . . . my Mother!
> My God! My God! Don't forget my Mother![16]

Arriving in San Francisco near the middle of February, Guerrero and Manrique found jobs as stevedores on the docks and worked there until the end of September 1905. In San

Francisco, Guerrero's increasing social and political concerns became more clear when he published a small periodical entitled *Alba Roja*, advocating workers' causes and radical ideas. In September the two friends left California to be closer to Mexico, seeking employment in the copper mines of Arizona. They learned there was a great demand for Mexican workers in Morenci, Arizona. They quickly found work in the Detroit Copper Mining Company smelter in Morenci. Just a few days after his arrival Práxedis wrote his mother that although he had opportunities to go to other areas, he thought he would stay in Morenci indefinitely—it was a good place to work.[17] He worked in Morenci over a year and a half—a time when he would begin to organize workers, edit a periodical, affiliate with the *Partido Liberal Mexicano* of Ricardo Flores Magón, and become an outspoken enemy of Porfirio Díaz. It was a very significant time for Guerrero. To understand his transformation into a *revoltoso*, however, the reader should know something of the development of the *magonista* movement.

THE MAGONISTAS AGAINST THE PORFIRIATO

The opposition movement to the government of Porfirio Díaz that originated around the turn of the century—although organized as the *Partido Liberal Mexicano (PLM)*—would come to be identified with Ricardo Flores Magón and has been studied extensively and intensively. In recent years, it might even be said that Flores Magón is more widely recognized in Mexico than the man he worked so hard and so long to unseat. Since Práxedis Guerrero spent the last few years of his short life serving the *magonista* cause, and since almost all his published writings were in the same cause, some understanding of the movement's origins and ideology is necessary.[1]

While scattered demonstrations and other expressions of discontent with the continued reelections of Porfirio Díaz appeared in the early 1890s, meaningful opposition did not develop until 1900. In San Luis Potosí, Camilo Arriaga, an engineer from a prestigious and politically important family, organized a movement to call attention to the way Mexico had strayed from the ideals of nineteenth century liberalism symbolized by Benito Juárez and the Constitution of 1857. Of particular concern to Arriaga was Catholic leaders' flaunting of restrictions on the Church. Both social and political reasons drove middle-class intellectuals in San Luis Potosí to question the Díaz regime. Economic difficulties in the area beginning in the 1890s further fueled disenchantment. Joining Arriaga in founding the liberal movement or responding to its call were numerous fellow *potosinos* like Antonio Díaz Soto y Gama, Juan Sarabia, and Librado Rivera, all of whom would play important roles in the years to come. In 1900 Arriaga put out a call to like-minded men throughout Mexico to meet in San Luis Potosí to consider action to organize the growing dissent. It was this call that brought Flores Magón into the movement.[2]

Ricardo Flores Magón, the second of three brothers between Jesús and Enrique, had come from his native Oaxaca to study law in Mexico City.[3] Leaving law school for opposition journalism, Ricardo, with Jesús and others, had started a periodical, *Regeneración*, dedicated at first to publicizing and criticizing bad or unfair administration of justice in Mexico. The early condemnations were a short step away from direct attacks on the Díaz regime, which obviously controlled the administration of justice. These activities brought Ricardo, as chief editor, to the attention of the San Luis Potosí group, and he was invited to attend the first liberal congress, which would meet in that city on February 5, 1901. Although a majority of those in attendance did not support Flores Magón's increasingly sharp attacks on the Díaz government, *Regeneración* became something of the official paper of the new *Partido Liberal Mexicano* formed at the meeting.

The budding opposition came to the attention of government authorities, both state and national, of course, and repressive acts followed. Arriaga's initial call resulted in the formation of liberal clubs throughout the republic. Many of them were silenced.

Bernardo Reyes—by this time *PLM's* much hated, staunch enemy—led the first attack on Liberals in Lampazos, Nuevo León, only a few months before Guerrero joined the Second Military Reserve. Means of suppression included using the legal system to shut down the opposition press. The Flores Magóns and others were arrested several times, for example, and *Regeneración*, after having been printed first in Mexico City, later in San Luis Potosí, and again in the capital was abandoned in 1901. Some issues of *Regeneración* had been printed on the presses of *El Diario del Hogar*, the periodical Guerrero represented in León. *El Diario del Hogar* was shut down briefly.

Although a dispirited Jesús Flores Magón left the movement, Ricardo, joined by younger brother Enrique, and others, resumed opposition journalism every time Ricardo was released from confinement. Arriaga, Díaz Soto y Gama, Sarabia, and Rivera also published an anti-Díaz paper, *El Demófilo*, in San Luis Potosí, and had also been jailed for their efforts. While there is no indication that Guerrero was familiar with *Regeneración* before he went to the United States, he had seen copies of *El Demófilo*. In July 1902, Ricardo took over direction of *El Hijo del Ahuizote*, which previously had been known for satirical political cartoons. This did not stop the arrests but ultimately almost all the *PLM* leadership would come to congregate in the offices of *El Hijo del Ahuizote*—when Ricardo was in jail, Juan Sarabia edited the paper. Finally, in April 1903, about the time Guerrero renounced his position in the Second Military Reserve, a raid on the newspaper offices in Mexico City landed Ricardo and Enrique Flores Magón, Juan Sarabia, his cousin Manuel Sarabia, and Librado Rivera in prison.

The few not arrested clandestinely used one press after another to keep the paper going—*El Hijo* was followed by *El*

Padre, then *El Nieto* and finally by *El Bisnieto del Ahuizote*, but soon all were shut down. The Mexican Supreme Court carried the suppression to the limit by ratifying a lower court order that prohibited the circulation of any publication which contained Flores Magóns' writings. When Ricardo Flores Magón gained his release from prison in October 1903, he felt he could no longer carry on the struggle against the government while remaining in Mexico. He would have to leave the country. In early January 1904, he crossed into the United States at Laredo, Texas, some nine months before Práxedis Guerrero would leave the country, but perhaps some years ahead of his young follower-to-be in political ideology.4

Ricardo and Enrique Flores Magón and Juan and Manuel Sarabia were soon joined in Laredo by Arriaga and others. Because they had arrived without money, they received support from sympathizers in the Texas border town. It would be some time, however, before they could generate resources to publish *Regeneración* again. They moved to San Antonio to begin the second era of *Regeneración* in November 1904. After a December assassination attempt on Ricardo, however, revealed that the San Antonio police would not protect them (in fact, the police would conspire against them), the Liberals decided they might still be too close to Mexican soil. Certainly, Mexican authorities were well aware of their actions. They moved to St. Louis, Missouri, early in 1905, helped in the process by a loan from Coahuilan hacendado Francisco I. Madero, who would turn away from the movement years before initiating the Revolution of 1910. St. Louis was chosen because recent arrival, and adherent to the cause, Antonio I. Villarreal, from Lampazos, Nuevo León, had contacts in that city. *Regeneración*, which was being distributed widely in Mexico, appeared for the first time in the Missouri city in February 1905.

In September 1905, in a significant move, the Mexican expatriates formed the *Junta Organizadora del Partido Liberal Mexicano*, with Ricardo Flores Magón as president; Juan

Sarabia, vice-president; Villarreal, secretary; Enrique, treasurer. The other board members, or *vocales*, were Manuel Sarabia, Rosalío Bustamante, and Librado Rivera. The Flores Magóns were from Oaxaca and Villarreal was from Nuevo León, but the rest were from San Luis Potosí. But *potosino* influence waned as political differences between Flores Magón and Arriaga, which had surfaced several times, soon drove Arriaga from the movement. It cannot be said with any certainty that Flores Magón had embraced anarchism at this time, but he was clearly pursuing a more radical course than Arriaga was comfortable with. His concern for workers and peasants, along with increasingly explicit calls for revolt in Mexico alienated the Maderos, Arriagas, and most of the other upper class liberals and intellectuals. Práxedis Guerrero would be an obvious exception when he joined the movement later, but by then he had adopted the lifestyle of a worker.

Regeneración reached a circulation of 20,000, most being sent into Mexico—later smuggled into Mexico when steps were taken to prevent its distribution. New opposition, a satirical paper from Mexico, *El Colmillo Público*, strongly supported the liberal effort. Mexican authorities were concerned enough about the influence of the *magonistas* to send a Oaxacan government functionary to St. Louis in October 1905 to bring libel and defamation charges against the editors. St. Louis police and private detectives arrested the Flores Magóns and Juan Sarabia, confiscating and selling all their property. *El Colmillo Público* led the fund-raising efforts to put *Regeneración* on the presses again. The junta leaders, released from jail in January 1906, feared efforts to extradite them to Mexico on other charges. Consequently, in March 1906, they jumped bond and fled to Canada, leaving Villarreal, Rivera, and Manuel Sarabia to publish the paper in St. Louis.[5]

Almost from the first the *PLM* movement was thoroughly infiltrated. United States authorities were eager to cooperate with the Mexican government in keeping tabs on the comings and goings of the *magonistas*. United States postal authorities were especially cooperative, making it difficult to maintain second class mailing privileges, but, more importantly, postal workers turned over all correspondence to and from the junta to government officials or to private detectives hired by Mexican authorities. A number of detective agencies would be used over the next several years, but clearly the most significant was the Thomas Furlong Detective Agency of St. Louis, employed by the Mexican consul in that city. Furlong himself would devote two years of full-time work to the *magonistas*.[6]

The second half of 1906 was a most eventful time for the PLM, even with much of the junta leadership in hiding or on the run. In July, the Liberals would publish their program and manifesto calling for revolution, and in the fall of 1906 they would attempt to launch a revolt in Mexico. Even before these developments, the *magonistas* were blamed by Mexican officials for one of the most serious labor conflicts in modern Mexican history—the strike and riot at the Cananea Consolidated Copper Company in Cananea, Sonora, in June 1906. Cananea is near the Arizona border and the principal owner of the copper company was the American entrepreneur William C. Greene. One of the major grievances in the dispute was the disparity in pay between Mexican and American workers. There were numerous other concerns but company officials refused to discuss them or to recognize any of the workers' organizations. A conflict erupted, panic and fear of race war ensued, and Arizona Rangers and other "volunteers" from Arizona Territory were allowed to cross the border to help restore order. Mexican federal troops and rural police, the famed *rurales*, led by Emilio Kosterlitski, quickly brought an end to the conflict.

The fact that this occurred so close to the United States and that *norteamericanos* were permitted to violate Mexican national sovereignty proved acutely embarrassing to the Díaz government. To try to overcome some of this embarrassment Mexican officials went to great lengths to place the blame on "outside agitators"—particularly the *PLM*. As a matter of fact, the activities of the *magonistas* was well known to many of the workers in Cananea and among the key organizers trying to establish unions were several followers of the liberal movement. *Regeneración* was circulated in Cananea and read widely by the workers. There was no direct involvement by any of the St. Louis junta, however, in the events leading up to the conflict at Cananea. Ironically, publicity generated by the accusations of the Mexican government gave the *PLM* greater status in many areas. Three days after the Cananea strike broke out, for example, Práxedis Guerrero formed a workers' organization in Morenci, Arizona, and asked to affiliate with the junta.7

The events in Cananea also focused more attention on the *Programa y Manifesto* of the *Junta Organizadora del Partido Liberal Mexicana*, published on July 1, 1906. Issued from St. Louis, it was the first extensive indictment of the Porfiriato: the manifesto called for revolution, and laid out plans for post-Díaz Mexico. The Program of the Mexican Liberal Party is a basic document of modern Mexican history, with historians and social scientists still debating its influence on later constitutional development. Although published in St. Louis at a time when the principal junta leaders were in Canada, the *Programa y Manifesto* is generally considered to be the work of Ricardo Flores Magón, Juan Sarabia, and Antonio I. Villarreal, the three most active and able writers on the junta. Ideas came from many sources, including many in Mexico, as both *Regeneración* and *El Colmillo Público* had solicited suggestions in earlier issues. The *PLM* Program was liberal, reformist, and nationalistic. It contained extensive provisions dealing with social welfare and labor issues, but in many respects it was a call for a return to many of the tenets of Juárez liberalism modified with features from contemporary socialist thought. Though the Constitution of 1917 did not go as far in some areas as this 1906 agenda, it still did not represent the more radical views Flores Magón himself held by this

Mexican worker in the Douglas, Arizona, smelter about 1906. (Courtesy Arizona Historical Society/Tucson.)

time. It was, however, a program for a revolution that the *PLM* leaders thought they were on the verge of launching.[8]

The revolt of 1906, widely and erroneously thought to be scheduled for Mexican Independence Day, September 16, was to consist of attacks across the border by Mexicans from the United States and coordinated with uprisings directed by *PLM*-affiliated clubs throughout Mexico. With the *PLM* leadership in the U.S., it was logical to depend on *revoltosos* in the United States to carry the fight to Mexico. Also, it was easier to arm such groups. Success, however, would ultimately depend on the participation of rebels in Mexico, and the *magonistas* were depending heavily on the liberal clubs that had sprung up in response to Arriaga's 1900 call. They were the subscribers to *Regeneración*, the ones who had responded to calls for funds to support the movement, the people who had submitted suggestions for the *Programa*. On both sides of the border, however, the movement was thoroughly infiltrated by agents hired by Mexico, and both national governments were prepared to resist. A 1906 revolution was doomed.

Two principal sites in the United States were targeted by the Liberals as staging points for the revolt—the border town of Douglas, Arizona Territory, where Antonio de P. Araujo had organized a club in 1905, and the State of Texas, particularly around El Paso and Del Rio. In Arizona, liberal activity had centered around Araujo, who would be a major figure later in Texas. Araujo, however, was no longer in the Arizona in 1906; Tomás Espinosa was the local *PLM* leader. Miners and other Mexican workers in the area, targeting Sonoran border cities, would make the assault. Although no specific date had been set, Flores Magón and the other junta leaders had issued commissions and written letters discussing plans and strategies for the invasion. An agent of the Sonoran governor infiltrated the movement and when his reports were turned over to United States officials, Arizona Rangers and other law enforcement officers arrested the conspirators in early September 1906. Several were tried and convicted of neutrality law violations and others were deported to Mexico, where they were tried and convicted of various charges. The commissions and letters from the junta also served as the basis for the later arrest, hearings, trial, and conviction of Ricardo Flores Magón and other junta leaders.[9] The removal of these *PLM* leaders would put Práxedis Guerrero in a prominent role. Guerrero was in Arizona in 1906 though there is no evidence that he played any part in the proposed revolt that year.[10]

Although activities in Arizona led to the evidence for the trial and conviction of the *magonista* leaders, Flores Magón, Juan Sarabia, and Villarreal went to Texas to direct the revolt. In early September they gathered in the home of Lauro Aguirre in El Paso. Aguirre, publisher of *La Reforma Social,* was a vocal critic of the Díaz government and a sympathizer of the liberal cause, but not an active leader as Mexican officials believed. Prisciliano G. Silva was the *PLM* leader in El Paso and directed preparations for the revolt in that area. At Del Rio, farther down the Río Grande, Crescencio Villarreal Márquez, publisher of yet another newspaper, *1810,* was the designated delegate of the *PLM* junta. He was charged with rallying support in the neighboring state of Coahuila. In all areas funds were short and acquiring arms and mustering men to bear them were not easy tasks.[11]

In El Paso, Flores Magón and Sarabia drafted a proclamation for rebel groups to distribute when the revolt began. A justification for taking up arms, the proclamation also called for support of the Liberal Party Program and urged Mexican soldiers to come over to the cause.[12] September 16 came and went with no revolt, but ten days later Juan José Arredondo, commissioned by Márquez in Del Rio, led a force of about sixty men against Jiménez, Coahuila. Initially successful, the rebels were counterattacked by Mexican federal troops and defeated, most survivors fleeing back across the United States border to Texas. Mexican authorities dismissed the attack as the work of bandits, saying the "affair had no political significance." United States officials differed in refusing to extradite Arredondo and others because the attack was considered a political offense. Deportation proceedings also failed.[13]

Other than the Coahuila frontier, the only other area where the revolt produced action was far to the south in the state of Veracruz. Hilario C. Salas was the liberal leader in Veracruz and, despite constant harrassment from government authorities, planned to join the uprising in 1906. Although he knew that a revolt from the north was unlikely, in late September Salas issued the proclamation he had received from El Paso. Raising a force of approximately 1,000, many of whom were dispossessed indigenous peasants seeking to recover their lands, Salas proposed to attack the towns of Acayucán, Minititlán, and Puerto México. Salas personally led the assault on Acayucán, the only part of the plan carried out. When Salas was wounded, the attack fell apart and federal troops were able to rout the rebels in all three areas. Reprisals were carried out against a number of villages, and most of the leaders were captured, tried, and sentenced to terms in the Veracruz fortress prison, San Juan de Ulúa. Salas escaped capture.[14]

The uprising in Veracruz could not be easily dismissed as the work of bandits, but the Mexican government felt the source of all the trouble was the junta in the United States. *Regeneración*, still publishing from St. Louis, was directed largely by Librado Rivera, the only member of the junta in the city. In September, *Regeneración* was effectively silenced when St. Louis authorities seized all the Liberals' property. The basis of this action was a libel suit brought by William C. Greene, the Cananea copper magnate who became obsessive in his hostility toward the Mexican radicals. Soon Rivera was arrested and a week later Aaron López Manzano, a *Regeneración* typesetter, was also picked up. Both men were secretly taken to Ironton, Missouri, about seventy-five miles south of St. Louis, and held incommunicado for three weeks while the Mexican government worked to have them extradited. Word of the arrests reached the St. Louis press and a storm of publicity led to the release of the men. Rivera fled the city, rejoining Flores Magón the next year in California.[15]

Before Rivera's flight, action had finally been taken against the junta leaders gathered in El Paso. Enrique Creel, governor of Chihuahua, had received the reports that the Furlong Detective Agency was then providing and knew that Flores Magón, Sarabia, and others were in the area. Creel asked Díaz to send more troops to Ciudad Juárez, across the river from El Paso. Once in Ciudad Juárez, the Mexican military leader was able to send officers to infiltrate the movement in that city. The Mexican consul in El Paso was informed by both the infiltrators on the Mexican side and the detective reports on the United States side. On October 19, El Paso police arrested Antonio I. Villarreal, Lauro Aguirre, and the chief arms contrabandist, José Cano. The next day Mexican officials arrested Juan Sarabia and others in Ciudad Juárez. More arrests followed, but Ricardo Flores Magón, the "soul of everything," narrowly escaped capture and fled the city.

With the Mexican government offering $20,000 for his capture, Flores Magón was in flight or in hiding for many months, pursued by Furlong detectives, United States Department of Justice agents, and postal authorities. Probably he spent most of the time in California. He went first to Los Angeles, then to San Francisco, and later to Sacramento, where he was rejoined by Villarreal. The Mexican government had been eager to get Villarreal back to Mexico, and after his arrest in El Paso hoped deportation proceedings would send him back. Extradition efforts would doubtless fail, and charges of neutrality law violations could land him in a United States prison, but getting him back to Mexico was clearly the goal. In February 1907, however, when it seemed Villarreal was destined to be sent back, he escaped from Texas authorities and fled to California.[16]

The only junta member who did not slip out of the grasp of officials was Juan Sarabia. He was tried and convicted in

Chihuahua, but not before he was able to make a dramatic and moving statement in his own defense, attacking the Porfiriato in very strong language. Sarabia was sentenced to seven years in San Juan de Ulúa. Other arrests and suppressions followed in Mexico and many liberal supporters in Mexico City also ended up in the Veracruz prison, along with those captured in Coahuila, Chihuahua, and Veracruz, as well as several deported from Arizona and Texas. In early 1907 Flores Magón and Villarreal issued a circular letter from California, recounting the events of 1906 and appealing for funds to reestablish *Regeneración*. Still failing to realize how completely the movement had been infiltrated, Flores Magón attributed the failures of 1906 to betrayals within the ranks.[17]

In June the Liberals began a new paper in Los Angeles; instead of *Regeneración*, the periodical was entitled *Revolución*. Modesto Díaz was the editor of record, but major input came from Flores Magón, who moved to Los Angeles toward the end of June. Villarreal and Rivera—junta and *Regeneración* veterans—joined him there. The whereabouts of the junta leadership was still of great concern to Mexico. One member, Manuel Sarabia, was in Douglas, Arizona, working on a local newspaper. He had been important in getting Práxedis Guerrero involved with the *PLM* and soon would have Guerrero contributing to *Revolución*.[18]

Earlier, Sarabia had been the central figure in an outlandish kidnapping that would deeply affect *magonista* attitudes and fears in dealing with United States and Mexican legal authorities. At the end of June, Sarabia was arrested by Arizona Rangers. The Mexican consul, the Rangers, and the local police conspired to take Sarabia from the jail and hand him over to Emilio Kosterlitski and Mexican *rurales* on the Mexican side of the border. Word of what had happened got out and there were protests from the local press, citizens' committees, labor organizers, and civil libertarians. In less than two weeks Sarabia was returned to United States by embarrassed Mexican officials, who attempted to shift blame to local interests. The Sarabia case would continue to be important to the Liberals; future arrests of *PLM* leaders would carry the fear of being forcefully taken to Mexico to face death or imprisonment.[19]

Certainly this fear was present when the pursuit finally caught up with Flores Magón less than two months after the arrest and kidnapping of Sarabia. Thomas Furlong had located the *revoltoso* in Los Angeles and had notified his Mexican employers on August 21, 1907. This had not required great detective work since a San Francisco newspaper had carried an article almost two weeks earlier that Flores Magón was publishing *Revolución* in Los Angeles. The article had even included his address. Enrique Creel travelled to Los Angeles to oversee the arrest of his long-sought enemy. On August 23, Furlong, one of his agents and a number of Los Angeles police officers—some also on Mexico's payroll—arrested Flores Magón, Villarreal, and Rivera.[20]

The arrest, which came only after a struggle, marked the beginning of a crucial three-year period in the *PLM* battle against the Porfiriato. Eventually charged with violations of neutrality laws, the three captives would fight extradition for a year and a half but trial and conviction in Arizona would keep them in United States prisons for another eighteen months. Flores Magón tried to keep the revolutionary movement alive from behind bars but had limited success.

A crisis of leadership faced the liberal cause and one of the key figures who stepped in to fill the void was Práxedis G. Guerrero.

ON BECOMING A REVOLUTIONARY

The role of a leader of the *Partido Liberal Mexicano* in the United States was not something Práxedis Guerrero sought for himself. Instead, it was a position he assumed out of necessity and one he achieved as his talents became obvious. Because Guerrero's responsibilities grew quietly, they remained relatively unknown long after he had taken charge. Mexican authorities and the private detectives in their employ and United States national, state, and local government officials continued to concentrate on other prominent figures in the PLM. When they finally realized Guerrero's importance in the *magonista* cause, they could not catch him. Guerrero was the only significant leader who was never arrested, despite mighty efforts to do so.

Guerrero first affiliated with the *PLM* while working in Morenci, Arizona, where he came into contact with junta member Manuel Sarabia, who told him of the ideas and work of the *Junta Organizadora del Partido Liberal Mexicano*. How and where Guerrero first met Sarabia is not known, but, despite occasional disagreements, they became close friends. After contacts with Sarabia, and just after the outbreak of conflict at Cananea, Guerrero formed an organization of Mexican workers at Morenci to encourage liberal ideals. Francisco Manrique and Manuel Vázquez, who had come to the United States with Guerrero from Guanajuato, joined Práxedis in the movement.[1]

The group they started was called *Obreros Libres*. They indicated in a brief constitution that they organized to support the *PLM* in working for the "regeneration of the fatherland." Further, after emphasizing their fight against the "tyranny of the dictatorship," they affirmed: "Social reform and political reform of Mexico are the ideals for which we are now and will always be ready to sacrifice all our energies. The people's cause is ours." Among the nine officers signing the document were Guerrero as president, Vázquez as secretary, and Manrique as a member of the executive committee. A copy of the document, along with subscriptions to *Regeneración*, was sent to the junta in St. Louis later that same month. The Flores Magóns and Juan Sarabia were in Canada at the time but in mid-July Antonio I. Villarreal forwarded to Guerrero a letter of welcome from Ricardo Flores Magón and an official welcome from the junta signed by Flores Magón, president, and Villarreal, secretary.[2]

Flores Magón's letter to his "correligionist," the term of address used by the liberals, urged him to work diligently to help achieve the the Liberal Party Program. He also assured Guerrero that ideas and suggestions from the Arizona group would be welcome and would receive serious consideration. The formal welcome praised the ideals of the *Obreros Libres*, but concluded with a rather dramatic exhortation: "Correligionists: Don't lose courage. Perhaps heaven has already prepared the laurel wreath that will encircle our fighters' foreheads. Forward!" As the preparations for the attempted revolt of 1906 went on, Guerrero received more communications from Flores Magón, mostly dealing with collecting of funds and difficulties of communications. Flores Magón did write that "the hour of national justice is rapidly approaching," but there is no indication that Guerrero participated directly in the uprising.[3]

Guerrero worked in Morenci until June 1907 when he moved to Douglas, Arizona, where he began work at a copper mine. He attempted to return to Morenci, but the shop foreman told him he could not rehire him on orders of the superintendent because he was a member of the Western Federation of Miners, a radical labor movement feared and hated by mine owners in the western United States. The foreman told Guerrero he could help him get a job in Clifton, Arizona, but Práxedis chose to return to Douglas. In fact, he was not a member of the Western Federation of Miners, but his activities on behalf of workers were becoming known to the mine operators.

His parents in Guanajuato were already concerned about their son and when one Cristóbal Espinosa, recently returned from the United States, told the Guerreros that Práxedis was "going astray and had been fired from his job in Morenci because of bad behavior," their anxieties increased.[4] Guerrero wrote home: "What ugly things could Cristóbal Espinosa say about me? This individual was sometimes with me, in my house and in the shop where I worked in Morenci, and is witness to my life as a worker; he can say that he saw me in a humble room, in company of Francisco Manrique, who, as you know, came with me; he can say that many times he saw me blackened by smoke, dirty, and full of oil, but he can never say that he saw me doing something bad." After explaining to his parents some of the things he had been doing on behalf of the workers and why he could not return to Morenci, Guerrero concluded: "That groundless accusation of belonging to the Western Federation, enemy of the Company, was made by a contemptible fellow. Perhaps Cristóbal referred to this and gave it a bad interpretation. Tell me what the man said and I will tell you what is true."5

In Douglas, as in Morenci, Guerrero continued to work, always living on what he earned. As an early biographer, Martínez Núñez, noted, for a person "born in silk diapers," it was remarkable the way Práxedis supported himself working in copper and coal mines, in wood-cutting, as a longshoreman, as a carpenter, in machine shops, and in railroad yards. Along with hard, physical labor and his organizing work, Guerrero continued to read and study. Favorite topics were histories of Mexico and of the French Revolution, ancient and modern philosophers, and increasingly socialist and anarchist theorists such as Errico Malatesta, Francisco Ferrer Guardia, Fernando Tarrida de Mármol, Mikhail Bakunin, and especially Pyotr Kropotkin. He was becoming something of an apostle of the latter, emphasizing the ideology of mutual aid, equality, and respect.6

Guerrero was also drawn more and more into the activities of the liberal junta. Sarabia must have been instrumental in this as they shared a house in Douglas. When *Revolución* began publishing in Los Angeles in June 1907, Guerrero quickly began submitting material. Toward the end of June he was named a Special Delegate of the junta to work in Arizona. The commission came from Flores Magón, now in Los Angeles, although it was dated as if it came from St. Louis, still considered the home of the *PLM*. About this time Sarabia was kidnapped and taken to Mexico. Práxedis described the events later in a letter to his parents:

> One day Sarabia was apprehended because of the intrigues of the Mexican Consul. In the night he was kidnapped from the jail . . . and infamously delivered to the Mexican authorities of Sonora. The hateful circumstances in which this attack was committed outraged all people,

both Mexican and American, and there were strong protests and a citizens' committee asked for justice from the government in Washington. I, who had witnessed the crime, and knowing Sarabia incapable of killing anybody—this was the pretext the consul had used—and seeing that it was only an act of vengeance by the government—assuming that if he had been the culprit they would have extradited him legally—I wrote two loose leaf pages pointing out the culprits. Justice began to be done and Sarabia was brought back from Hermosillo and given his unconditional freedom here. Now we wait for the jury for the kidnappers. . . .7

The loose leaf pages Guerrero mentioned were distributed on the streets of Douglas and elsewhere and later published in *Revolución* under the title "Justice!" Guerrero attacked perpetrators on both sides of the border of the kidnapping but leveled his most virulent attack on Porfirio Díaz as the man behind it all. "The Mexican people must clean the Porfirian stain from their country," he wrote.[8] Such rhetoric quickly caught the attention of liberals throughout the Southwest. Later in July Manuel Sarabia, now free, wrote to his brother, Tomás Sarabia, in San Antonio, and explained the authorship of "Justice!" Apparently, Tomás thought the author was León Cárdenas, a liberal El Paso publisher. Manuel wrote that the work was not by Cárdenas but by Práxedis Guerrero. "The first is a little timid as a fighter, is my pal. The second is a fighter who knows no fear, is my friend and I am honored to call him my brother. Ah! If only we had many Guerreros!"[9]

August brought the arrests of Ricardo Flores Magón, Antonio Villarreal, and Librado Rivera in Los Angeles. Guerrero immediately began to assume a more prominent role, appealing for funds for the defense of the *PLM* leaders. His circular letter was dated August 31, 1907, and issued from Douglas, Arizona. Guerrero wrote: "The members of the *Junta Organizadora del*

Partido Liberal Mexicano have had to hide in the land of Lincoln, the country of great liberties, in order to fight for good and for Justice!" Although the liberals had the sympathy of the American public, they needed money—money for bail bonds and money for defense attorneys. A Douglas address was to be used for the collection of funds.[10]

Lázaro Gutiérrez de Lara, who had been working on *Revolución* from the beginning, took over major editorial responsibilities in Los Angeles. About a month later, however, he was arrested on rather vague charges and held over three months. In October 1907 Sarabia and Guerrero came to Los Angeles to take over for Gutiérrez de Lara in filling the editorial columns of *Revolución*. Sarabia acted as editor in chief and Guerrero ran the editorial staff. Enrique Flores Magón, who had been working in New York City since leaving brother Ricardo and Juan Sarabia in Canada a year earlier, also came to Los Angeles about the same time to rejoin the movement.[11]

Guerrero's family was aware of what had happened to the *magonista* leaders in Los Angeles and his mother wrote urging Práxedis to give up the "twisted road," which "could only lead him to disgrace, to prison, or to death." Práxedis replied in January 1908, writing:

> Don't see this with those fears, mamacita; to your eyes the difficulties and dangers are exaggerated. Calm yourself. What misfortune could survive that cannot be overcome by whomever works for the good of their fellow man? Is it wrong to search for the salvation of thousands of unfortunate creatures? You know what has occurred to my companions, but you ignore what their ceaseless work means for everyone. Much must I explain to you, but I will do it later, and then you will tell me if the road that I follow is honorable.
>
> I don't want, my mother, for you to grieve yourself; neither do I want you to condemn my labor, without hearing

me first.... I fervently wish to go speak to you, to show you my brain and my heart and to request your blessing in order to continue on this way that to you seems twisted, but I do not know if my thoughts will be fulfilled. To see my father, to see you and my brothers and sisters will be my desire and I will do all that is possible to achieve it....[12]

Before Guerrero went to Los Angeles, Manuel Sarabia was the only junta member he knew personally. In California he met Enrique Flores Magón immediately and became a close friend. In November 1907 Práxedis went to the Los Angeles County jail for his first meeting with Ricardo Flores Magón, Villarreal, and Rivera. In this and subsequent meetings Guerrero gained the complete confidence of Ricardo. Perhaps, it was, as Martínez Núñez suggested, that Ricardo saw Guerrero as the replacement for Juan Sarabia, the skilled writer languishing in prison in San Juan de Ulúa. In December 1907 Guerrero was elevated to second secretary of the junta. He, Manuel Sarabia, and Enrique were doing most of the editorial work on *Revolución*. Ricardo wrote to Sarabia on December 19, 1907: "*Revolución* is beautiful. I congratulate everyone and especially Práxedis. What a brilliant pen!"[13]

This outlet for Guerrero's pen proved to be short-lived. In January 1908 Manuel Sarabia was arrested on the same charges as the three jailed *magonistas*—violation of United States neutrality laws in connection with the 1906 aborted revolt in Arizona. Guerrero wrote Manuel's brother, Tomás, in San Antonio, with news of the arrest, telling him "If the ties of blood unite you with Manuel, no less strong are those that bind me to him: the brotherhood of ideas. If there are implacable enemies, there are also determined friends."[14] The following month the editor of record of *Revolución*, Modesto Díaz, and the printers, Federico Arizméndez and Fidel Ulíbarri, were arrested for the second time on libel suits brought by a Los Angeles police officer and the newspaper was suppressed.[15] Over the next three months Flores Magón, still in the Los Angeles County jail, wrote Guerrero several letters about possibilities of buying a new periodical, always essential to the movement. There were two existing papers Ricardo thought they might be able to acquire, *El Monitor Mexicano* and later *El Correo Mexicano*.

On March 8, 1908, he wrote Guerrero that they might be able to acquire *El Monitor*. Modesto Díaz, "well known already as an honest man," would be the editor. They could be sure that "the content of the newspaper will be absolutely in opposition to tyranny . . ." . But, Flores Magón told his young follower:

> We will need all the help you lend us in the editing of the newspaper. For our part, we will see if we can write something. I write with great difficulty. The posture in which I can do it is excessively uncomfortable and I had promised not to write for newspapers, but there is a need of writing and I will write, even if it is not much. You will bear most of the load; but if sometime we get out on bail we will alleviate your hard work.
>
> The newspaper is indispensable not only for our defense and to obtain resources for our defense by means of it, but to encourage those who are growing cold since they know nothing of the fight. Many believe that we are free and upon not seeing any manifestation of the struggle, they think that everything is finished. Others know that we are prisoners, but as they also notice that there is no struggle, because the secret works cannot be divulged, they must think that everything has been postponed and that there is no one outside of jail who continues in the work. In both cases there is the same result: discouragement.
>
> The newspaper is needed. This is understood by our own enemies, and so well, that they make every effort to leave the cause without a press. We have come to the United States, and are in the same condition as in Mexico, without the freedom to write.

Once they acquired a paper, Flores Magón urged Guerrero to "attack Díaz without compassion" but to be careful with the "characters of little importance" such as the police, judges, political bosses, and others who brought suits that kept the *magonista* press in trouble. "If we take care in dealing with these wretched ones, but we throw ourselves thoroughly into the fray when dealing with Porfirio Díaz and the big Mexican vampires, I believe that the newspaper will have a long life. . . ."16

A little over a week later Flores Magón wrote that the "purchase of the *Monitor* had fallen through, but *El Correo Mexicano* remains, and the owners are willing to sell it. Thus there is that hope of having a registered newspaper. . . ." Lack of funds eliminated that possibility, but Guerrero, assisted by Enrique Flores Magón, still tried to keep *Revolución* going. Toward the end of April, with the help of Modesto Díaz, they published a few more times. By the end of May, however, the small press was discovered and destroyed by police. Díaz, Arizméndez, and Ulíbarri were arrested again for libel. Díaz died in jail and *Revolución* died as well.17

Meanwhile, Guerrero was again beset with problems from home. Having learned that his father was gravely ill, he wrote on April 11, 1908, to a sister, "who knows if upon writing these lines my father will be in agony or his sufferings forever ended. . . . Many times I have traveled the space that stands between you and me; many times snatched by my thought I have gone to the head of my sick father, but . . . only my mere spirit keeps him company, while I uselessly search for the medium that will annihilate the distance. . . ."18 A week later José de la Luz Guerrero died and again Práxedis wrote his sister:

> Yes, your letter arrived after the news of my father's death; your letter that is not extensive in words but throbbing with feeling. It has made me feel the painful agony of our father. . . . Oh, why when someone close to my heart

suffers, why when the pain searches for one last victim, why am I not the chosen one?

How sad, how painful all this is; my father speaking to me during his last hours, and I, far away from him, was not able to have my voice reach him in his bed. . . . The wings of my thought could not really carry me up to where only the desire and the imagination could arrive. . .

It is twelve thirty, night time, when I am writing this and so many are the ideas, and so many the memories that wake in the still of my room, that I abandon the pen in order to meditate in the distant home, where you are, like I am, heart-stricken by the absence of father. . . .[19]

No matter how great the pain, Guerrero was too well known now to go to his mother and brothers and sisters without putting them in danger. Furthermore, the *PLM* leadership was hopeful once again of launching the revolt that would topple the Díaz regime and Guerrero expected to play a major role. Toward the end of May, Práxedis, accompanied by Francisco Manrique, left Los Angeles for El Paso, Texas, to contact the leaders of the coming insurrection and to gather arms (stored in the homes of Prisciliano G. Silva and José R. Aguilar) to support it. Guerrero hoped the revolt would involve raiders crossing the border from the United States, as well as coordinated uprisings throughout Mexico—the unrealized hopes in 1906.

Choosing the night of June 24-25, 1908—the anniversary of the infamous Díaz *"mátalos en caliente"* order to suppress an 1879 revolt in Veracruz—Guerrero sent representatives into Mexico to pass the word. Eugenio Anzalde and José Inés Salazar went into the border states of Sonora and Chihuahua. Práxedis sent Manrique to try to cover most of the rest of Mexico although there was virtually no money to support him. In a little more than three weeks, the resourceful Manrique did cover much of the Republic, returning to El Paso on June 24 in time to join the revolt himself—with fatal consequences. After Manrique left for

Mexico, Guerrero traveled along the border to pass on the date of the revolt to groups from Arizona to South Texas. He had advised the Flores Magóns of the date and he kept them informed of his movements. When he indicated he intended to cross into Chihuahua to prepare groups there, however, the Flores Magón brothers were alarmed.[20]

Enrique Flores Magón, still in hiding in Los Angeles, wrote to Guerrero:

> Listen to me Práxedis: I should be frank. I will tell you that I believe it is wrong and risky for you to go to Juárez before the movement; I would almost consider it an act that lacks wisdom. Remember what Ricardo always recommends and even begs of us, that we do not expose ourselves and risk falling into the hands of our enemies. And, thinking of the reasons Ricardo gives us, we must agree with him.
>
> Indeed, Práxedis, for the present, although we are anarchists, we should consider ourselves as leaders of the liberal army, and by our character as leaders, we should take care of ourselves to prevent the capture that would bring the chaos and confusion that Ricardo forebodes. The special circumstances which the movement is going through places us in the fight as leaders, and even as a flag to follow in combat and for which to fight. Don't believe by this, my good Práxedis, that megalomania has seized me. . . . No, I do not fail to recognize my poor aptitude as a leader, nor my lack of merit as a fighter in order to be taken as a flag; but at the same time, neither do our correligionists know us all personally, [and they] do not have the opportunity of studying and analyzing us. They believe that all in the Junta have the vigorous mental capacity of Ricardo or Juanito [Sarabia]. In any case, the point is, Práxedis, that if you or I or both at the same time fall into the hands of our enemies, it would bring discouragement, and even the dis-

bandment in our ranks, which, like the treason of Juárez, would bring failure of worse consequences than that of 1906.

We, Práxedis, should avoid all kind of failure. No matter that fools interpret our wisdom as cowardice; to hell with them and let us search for success. . . .

Enrique concluded that he would join Guerrero in El Paso, but for the moment "the lack of money prevents it. This irritates me and makes me worse than a scorpion, with pure rage, but this does not help. I continue here, and will continue here until the accursed poverty permits me to go and occupy my proper place near the events. . . ."[21] As events unfolded in the subsequent weeks, Flores Magón's letter proved to be more revealing than anyone might have imagined. Enrique finally made it to El Paso, traveling in the disguise of an Italian violinist and arriving just a few days before the revolt. But the *magonista* movement was infiltrated even more than it had been in 1906. Everything Ricardo attempted to smuggle out of the Los Angeles County Jail, even notes on dirty underwear, was intercepted. Mail between conspirators in the United States and mail to Mexico was copied for the benefit of the Mexican government. Crude codes and clever codes alike were broken. Mass arrests throughout Mexico killed any possibility of coordinated uprisings, even in Veracruz where the best Hilario C. Salas could do in 1908 was to promise to continue the fight.[22]

In El Paso, Enrique Flores Magón and Práxedis Guerrero managed to escape capture when local police, working closely with Ciudad Juárez authorities and the Mexican consul in El Paso, seized the accumulated arms and ammunition and arrested most of the conspirators. Prisciliano G. Silva, his son Benjamín, José María G. Ramírez, and Leocardio B. Treviño were all arrested and charged with violations of the neutrality law.[23] In 1908 the only places where the *PLM* initiated rebellions were in Viesca, Coahuila, a small town in the southern part of the state close to Torreón; Las Vacas, Coahuila, a border town across from Del Rio, Texas; and Palomas, Chihuahua, a small village near the New Mexico border, where Guerrero led the charge.

The revolt in Viesca began on the night of June 24 at the Hacienda Los Hornos. From there Benito Ibarra led about sixty rebels into town crying ¡*Abajo la dictadura!* and ¡*Viva el Partido Liberal!* Meeting little resistance the rebels opened the jails and took over the bank and the municipal presidency. They also attacked the home of the local *jefe político*, who was actually the target of local grievances. José Lugo, who had not been involved in setting off the revolt, emerged as the leading figure in what was a popular movement. The rebels held the town for about a day and a half before federal troops from Torreón and Saltillo converged on the area and drove the rebels from the nearby town of Matamoros to which they had fled and captured many in the process. Of those apprehended fifteen were tried and sentenced to terms ranging from three to twenty years in San Juan de Ulúa. Fifteen others received terms in local or area jails and prisons. Ibarra, the instigator, escaped capture, while Lugo, the leader after the revolt got underway, was sentenced to death and, after many delays, was executed in Saltillo on August 3, 1910.

Lugo became an important martyr for the *PLM* cause. Guerrero wrote later, "Lugo faced the consequences of his Libertarian actions without flinching . . . that young man, who scared the Judges with the greatness of his character, was awesome." When he was taken to a corral to be executed "they wanted to blindfold him, but he disdainfully rejected it; he stood firm, serene, without any alteration in his pulse, in front of the squad of pale soldiers, who discharged their weapons on his heroic chest." An American consular agent confirmed Guerrero's account.[24]

The *Partido Liberal Mexicano* was more directly involved in the attack on Las Vacas. Antonio de P. Araujo, who had been active in Arizona earlier, was the special delegate of the *PLM* in

Texas. He resided in Austin and Manuel Sarabia's brother, Tomás, who sometimes used the surname Labrada, lived in San Antonio. Sarabia edited a newspaper—*Reforma, Libertad y Justicia* (the *PLM* slogan)—that Araujo published from Austin beginning in May 1908. Araujo planned the attack on Las Vacas, although both men were involved in gathering and delivering the necessary arms. Command of the force was given to Encarnación Díaz Guerra, an officer who had left the Mexican federal army, and his second-in-command was Jesús M. Rangel. Between forty and sixty *revoltosos* joined the attack.

Early in the morning of June 26, Díaz Guerra led a three-pronged assault against federal positions. The battle raged for about five hours, with each side losing eight to ten killed and an equal number wounded. When the liberal forces began to run out of ammunition they withdrew, scattering back across the border or into the Coahuilan countryside. Because the incident occurred along the border, the press in the United States, especially in Texas, covered the attack extensively. Díaz Guerra, in true military fashion, submitted a complete formal report to the *PLM*. Guerrero later wrote such a detailed and dramatic account of the battle that many thought he had been a participant. His conclusion: "A failure, whisper some voices. An example, a lesson, encouragement, an immortal episode of a revolution that will triumph, says logic."[25]

Guerrero did participate in the final episode of the 1908 revolt, an attack on Palomas, Chihuahua, perhaps brought on by youthful impatience and frustration over the way revolutionary dreams had been shattered. After the arrests in El Paso, Guerrero and Enrique Flores Magón planned to cross the border and join other forces in an operation against Casas Grandes, Chihuahua. Flores Magón, taking his own advice about not getting caught, eliminated himself from combat by "accidentally" shooting himself between the toes. With liberal activity subdued in Casas Grandes, and most of the *PLM* sympathizers under arrest there, Guerrero and his small band moved on Palomas, about 100 kilo-

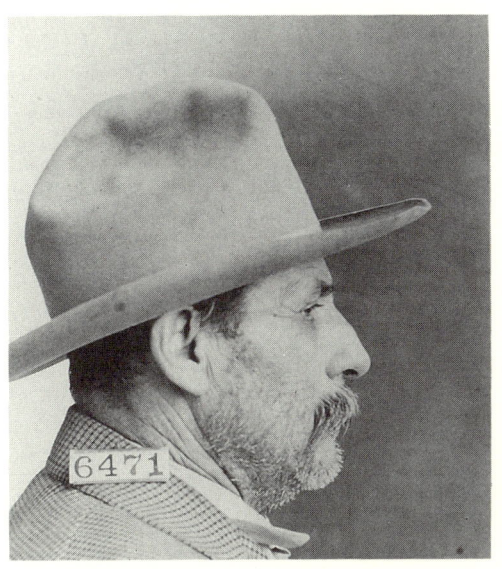

Encarnación Díaz Guerra (#6471) and Jesús María Rangel (#6927) were the leaders of the unsuccessful 1908 attack on Las Vacas, Coahuila. (Photos courtesy of the United States Department of Justice, Bureau of the Prisons.)

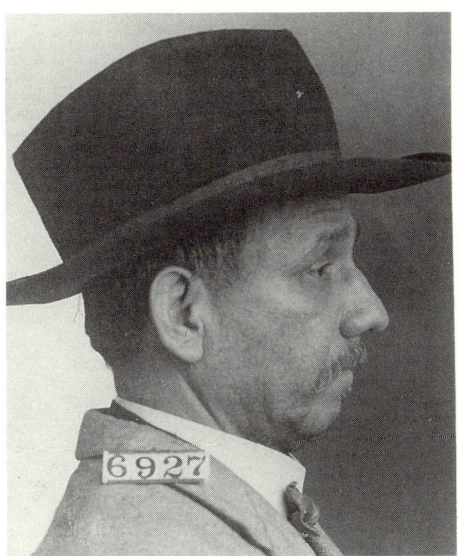

meters west of Juárez and not far from Columbus, New Mexico. Since Palomas was a customs station, there were about thirty fiscal agents and *rurales* there to defend the town. Guerrero's force consisted of himself, Francisco Manrique, and only nine others. "Eleven and not one more, to attempt, with an audacious move, to save the revolution which seemed to be shipwrecked in the surf of treachery and cowardice," wrote Práxedis.

Cutting the telegraph wires on the way into Palomas, the liberals attacked the customs station about 4 A.M., July 1, 1908. Armed with rifles and a few crude bombs, "rude weapons and homemade implements of warfare" according to the *Washington Post*, they turned from the empty station to the strongly defended headquarters of the *rurales*. In the assault the bombs proved to be too small. Francisco Manrique, advancing on the adobe structure, was mortally wounded. "The battle continued," Guerrero wrote, and "the bullets kept whistling from top to bottom and from bottom to top. The horizon was getting paler with the proximity of the sunshine, and Pancho [Manrique] was getting paler too, invaded by death, which kept advancing over his formerly proud, agile and daring body. The sun was rising, blending its brightness with that of a revolutionary star eclipsing." Manrique was the only fatality of the attack on Palomas, although Guerrero was wounded in the foot and the cheek. The liberals quit the fight, leaving the dying Manrique behind.

Manrique, described as a mere boy in some reports of the battle, refused to give his real name to the Mexican forces. As Práxedis wrote: "Pancho loved truth. He never lied to avoid a responsibility or to obtain a benefit. His word was frank and loyal, sometimes rude, but always sincere. And he who had always disdained the life and the welfare bought with falseness, died lying (a sublime lie), wrapped in the anonymity of a conventional name—Otilo Madrid—in order to save the revolution and his friends." Guerrero had begun his account of the attack on Palomas with these words: "This chapter in the history of freedom should be called *Francisco Manrique*; it should carry the name of that youth, almost a child, who died by the bullets of the tyranny on July 1, 1908, in the frontier village of Palomas."[26]

As in 1906, the Mexican government downplayed the insurrections of 1908 as simple bandit raids. Vice President Román Corral said, "this whole trouble has been caused by three irresponsible agitators and anarchists who are at present residing in the United States. These men, Enrique Flores Magón of Los Angeles, Thomas Sarabia of San Antonio, Texas, who goes by the name of Thomas Labrada, and Antonio P. Araujo of Austin, Texas, recently appealed to certain of the criminal and ignorant element of the border states of Mexico."[27] Even at this point, both Mexico and the United States, and their many public and private operatives, had not realized that the most important *insurrecto* bedeviling them was Práxedis Guerrero. With more arrests to follow the 1908 revolts, he would be practically the only one leading the struggle.

"A NOTORIOUS REVOLUTIONIST" — UNTIL IT KILLED HIM

From the unsuccessful, quixotic, attack on Palomas, which cost the life of his dear friend, Francisco Manrique, to his own death in Chihuahua in the waning days of 1910, Práxedis Guerrero was a man obsessed. It was as if the entire *Partido Liberal Mexicano* had come to rest on his shoulders. He traveled the borderlands from New Mexico, to Arizona, to Texas, to California, and back again. He went deep into Mexico for one last time. He went into the interior of the midwestern United States for the first time. He was working, writing, publishing, organizing, plotting, encouraging—all the while staying one step ahead of the myriad agents intent on arresting him.

After the attack on Palomas, Guerrero and his men went to Ciudad Guzmán, where they posed as miners—as indeed some of them were—on the way to Ciudad Juárez. After resting they went on to Juárez and crossed back into the United States at El Paso. Reuniting with Enrique Flores Magón and needing some rest and attention to his wounds, Guerrero accompanied Enrique to Albuquerque, New Mexico. From New Mexico, Flores Magón went to San Francisco where he found work as a mechanic in the American Can Company. Guerrero returned to Douglas, Arizona, before going on to El Paso, to try to organize revolutionary groups again.[1]

By this time, Mexican officials knew that Guerrero had led the Palomas raid and was a significant figure in the *magonista* movement. Consular agents along the border tried desperately to ferret out all the information they could about Guerrero. His earlier activities in Arizona, particularly his time in Morenci, came under close scrutiny. Since Guerrero had now been charged with neutrality law violations, he was subject to arrest wherever he went. However, no one knew him by sight the way most of the other *revoltosos* were known to police, federal agents, and private detectives hired by Mexico. The Mexican consul in Tucson, Arizona, tried without success to find a photograph of Práxedis. As luck would have it, the photo shop in Morenci had burned down two months earlier and "a young woman with whom said individual had relations, on being questioned by a person in her confidence who was sent for that purpose, answered with regret that she did not have a single photo of him. . . ."[2]

Always on the move, Guerrero rarely stayed put long enough to have a photo made. In Douglas, he met with Jesús M. Rangel, also a fugitive for his part in the raid on Las Vacas. They discussed the possibility of trying again in September 1908, but they decided to wait until 1909. Rangel was sent off to Oklahoma to work among the sizable population of Mexican miners in the Indian Territory, and to enlist support, raise funds, and acquire arms and ammunition for the cause. Rangel left Oklahoma in December after Encarnación Díaz Guerra, who had led the forces at Las Vacas, was arrested in the area. From Oklahoma, Rangel returned to San Antonio toward the end of December 1908. Andrea Villarreal González, sister of junta member Antonio Villarreal and probably the most prominent female follower of the *PLM*, had relocated from St. Louis to San Antonio. She helped Rangel reestablish contact with Guerrero, who by this time was in El Paso.

Meeting in the home of Prisciliano Silva, just released from Leavenworth Penitentiary for a neutrality law conviction, Rangel and Guerrero discussed the possibilities for revolution. Rangel returned to San Antonio to continue organizing; Guerrero went to San Francisco to tell Enrique Flores Magón what was happening. In February 1909, their appeals exhausted, Ricardo Flores Magón, Antonio I. Villarreal, and Librado Rivera were transferred from Los Angeles to Arizona Territory to stand trial for the neutrality law violations charged after the 1906 revolt. With the expectation that another attempt would be imminent in spite of their legal difficuties, the junta leaders decided that Guerrero should go to Mexico to assure *PLM* supporters in the central and southern parts of the Republic that triumph was in sight.[3]

Práxedis went directly to his native state of Guanajuato, staying first with relatives in León. Leaving early in the morning hours the next day with his brother, José, he returned to the highlands of his birth. Enroute, Práxedis stopped at the Manrique family ranch, Las Fundiciones. The family knew Francisco was dead but knew nothing of the circumstances. Following this sad duty, the greeting at the Guerrero family hacienda, Los Altos de Ibarra, was joyous and emotional. His mother, brothers, and sisters had not seen Práxedis in almost four and a half years. His appearance caused them some concern — the sometimes elegant dresser was attired as a common laborer. He was so thin his family thought he had been seriously ill. He assured them he was healthy, but that he no longer ate meat because "it hurt him that animals were sacrificed."4

Guerrero had changed in a number of ways that certainly did not fit with traditional Mexican hacienda life. He had considered his father something of a model hacendado who had increased the wages of the rural workers, paid them promptly, and did not exploit them at a *tienda de raya* (hacienda store). "Here is one of the estates where the *campesinos* are treated better," said Guerrero, "but it is not only this that I seek." A family servant told one of his sisters after his departure: "The master, don Práxedis, returned very changed, now he is very good; he would tell me not to call him master." His mother, observing his behavior, said "Práxedis is a saint, Práxedis is an angel."5

None of this made the family members eager, or even willing, to adopt the social and political ideas which Práxedis so earnestly spoke of. Still, they helped. After efforts to convince him to give up his activities and stay at Los Altos de Ibarra failed, one sister and two brothers accompanied him to central and southern Mexico to arouse less suspicion as he traveled. On February 22, 1909, Práxedis parted for the final time, leaving his mother and four brothers and sisters at the train station in León. On his departure, he renounced his inheritance, saying, if he did not return, his possessions should be distributed to the most needy. It took him a little more than a week to complete his mission, traveling to Mexico City, Puebla, and Oaxaca. He sent his mother a postcard from Chihuahua and bid farewell to the sister and brothers who were with him in Ciudad Juárez.6

Meanwhile, the search for Guerrero in the United States intensified. Since the raid on Palomas he had variously been reported in California, Arizona, New Mexico, and Texas. One report had him going to Mexico in July 1908 with John Kenneth Turner and Lázaro Gutiérrez de Lara, the trip that resulted in Turner's historic *Barbarous Mexico* articles and book.7 With Ricardo Flores Magón still safely locked up, the Mexican government decided that after 1908 it could do without the services

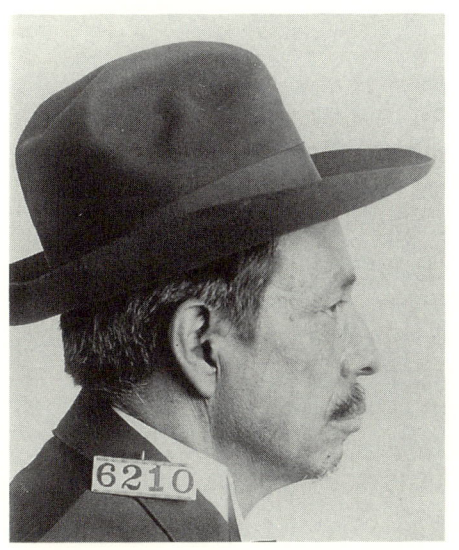

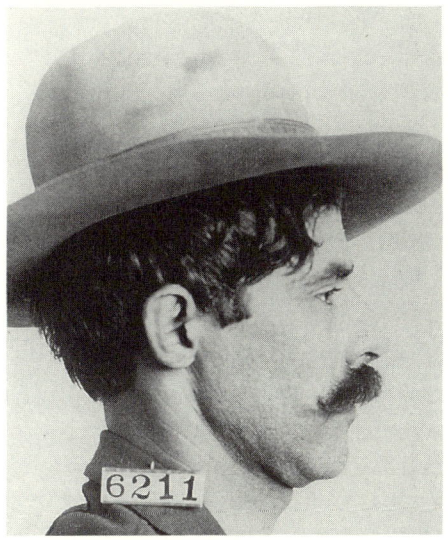

Prisciliano G. Silva (#6210), Antonio de P. Araujo (#6307), and Leocardio B. Treviño (#6211) were three prominent revoltosos *who eagerly followed Guerrero. (Photos courtesy United States Department of Justice, Federal Bureau of Prisons.)*

of Thomas Furlong and his St. Louis detective agency. Furlong thought he might keep the steady work Mexico had afforded for two years by going after Guerrero and Enrique Flores Magón. He wrote:

> The United States authorities at this time are very anxious to apprehend Enrique Flores Magón and P. G. Guerrero, and you will doubtless recollect that I reported to you about a year ago that I could have apprehended Enrique Flores Magón at Los Angeles, California, and asked for instructions regarding his apprehension and was notified by wire not to cause his apprehension at that time. He and Guerrero are now together and are migrating between points in Arizona and Los Angeles, Cal., and both are wanted by United States Attorney Boynton at the present time and against whom he has secured indictments in Texas, and I have no doubt that we could locate them in a very short time if desired by your government.[8]

It was never quite that easy with Guerrero. The Mexican consul in Los Angeles paid special agents and supplemented the pay of Los Angeles city police trying to catch him in the fall of 1908; Arizona consular agents enlisted the aid of private detectives.[9] With all this effort, it is surprising that no one chasing Práxedis seemed to be aware that he made the trip to Mexico in February 1909. On his return to the United States, Guerrero traveled into the midwestern states of Kansas, Missouri, and Illinois, again undetected. The purpose of this trip was to convince Julius Haldeman, editor of the widely read Kansas socialist weekly *The Appeal to Reason*, to provide more information about the goals of the PLM. Eugene V. Debs, the United States socialist leader who had written about the liberal cause in the Kansas paper, also was interested in learning more. With Ricardo Flores Magón, Villarreal, and Rivera on trial in Arizona, and with new trials pending from the 1908 revolt, the *magonistas* needed both financial and popular support. It was critical to keep American socialists on their side.¹⁰

In May 1909 the three junta leaders on trial in Arizona were convicted and sentenced to eighteen months in the territorial prison. Returning from his sojourn to the midwest, Guerrero knew he would have to bear the burden of leadership for the liberals. He returned to Texas, going first to San Antonio, then dividing his time between that city and El Paso. In July the Mexican consul in El Paso said he had met Guerrero, knew where he was living and working, but could not get the United States deputy marshal to make the arrest because no one could provide positive identification. The consul did not have the funds to bring anyone from Arizona who could do it.¹¹

In San Antonio Guerrero worked with Jesús Rangel and Tomás Sarabia to collect arms and ammunition for a new assault on the Porfiriato. It was not simply Díaz that he was fighting at this point. He told Rangel:

> when we resolved to fling ourselves into the fight it is because we have ideas very well placed in our heads. The man who thinks and feels the ideas, does not fear sacrifices: he goes to them willing to give his life. You must have seen that I am uncompromising, that many times I argue details; that I appear obstinate and meticulous, and that I am not in conformity with the disciplined organization of the rebellious groups. I believe that a popular revolution should be spontaneous, without leaders. If I address you in this manner, it is because I believe that you truly love liberty. . . . I am not a mere political enemy of General Díaz. I am an anarchist; I don't fight because I hate government, but for the love of a free humanity. . . . Our revolution must show the manner of liberating and not of governing.¹²

Shortly afterward, Rangel and Sarabia were arrested in a raid directed by United States Deputy Marshal Fred H. Lancaster.

Rangel was already under indictment for violation of the neutrality laws for his part in the attack on Las Vacas, Coahuila, in 1908. Now, both men were charged and the raid produced documents regarding efforts to buy arms, as well as considerable correspondence from Guerrero outlining his role in the *PLM*. Included was a mainfesto signed by Guerrero and Enrique Flores Magón, dated May 10, 1909, and likely written by Guerrero. It was from the "Revolutionary Council" and directed toward Mexican workers, and other "workers," recounting the actions of Díaz and his foreign capitalist allies to exploit workers and persecute their champions. "It is not alone in Mexico that we are brutally treated by the authorities, for in the United States we are treated like beasts," the manifesto proclaimed.[13]

Guerrero had been writing letters and issuing manifestos and proclamations, but he had not had a regular forum for his work since the final suppression of *Revolución* in May 1908. The lack of such an outlet probably bothered him as much as it had Ricardo Flores Magón. Back in El Paso, about the same time Rangel and Sarabia were arrested, Guerrero published the inaugural issue of his first newspaper, *Punto Rojo*. The first issues were small four-page, "digest" size papers printed on a small press in the home of William Lowe, an El Paso socialist. Guerrero had "selected El Paso for geographical considerations, as being the most central point, where we could extend both north and south as well as east and west."[14] No matter how crude the appearance of the first issues, Práxedis again had a means of expressing his thoughts. He proclaimed beside the masthead of *Punto Rojo*: "I am not merchandise, I am an idea; and ideas are not bought, they are defended."[15]

Guerrero was working, as usual, to support himself; money never came easy. "Money is more scarce than the so-called one pound chick-peas," he had earlier written to a "correligionist" from San Antonio, or, as he called the city in another letter, "Hungryopolis."[16] The need to work, coupled with the ever present danger of arrest, meant that writing for *Punto Rojo* (circulated to liberal Texas supporters and often given away on the streets) was done hastily and Guerrero's lack of resources showed. As time went on, however, contributions came from Enrique Flores Magón and others, enabling Práxedis to improve both the size and the quality. To avoid problems for his family, in correspondence he called *Punto Rojo* his *chamaco*, his boy or youngster. In a letter to a sister he wrote, for example: "I believe that you have already received the third portrait of my youngster. It seems a little better than the others, but not as good as I would like. I plan to enlarge it; if I do, I will make two copies to send you one."[17]

The new periodical did not go unnoticed by the Mexican government. The consul in El Paso duly forwarded the very first issue to the Foreign Relations office in Mexico City, noting it had appeared "to increase the agitation," was "sold profusely," and was edited by Guerrero, "the *revoltoso* chief . . . mentioned frequently in my dispatches."[18] The consul believed it was being printed on the presses of Lauro Aguirre, the El Paso publisher who had so long been an outspoken critic of the regime of Porfirio Díaz. He believed *Punto Rojo* might hasten the arrest of Guerrero, but lamented the fact that the United States marshal in his district was old and not likely to be of much help.[19]

About a month later, on September 26, 1909, Arturo M. Elías, consul in Tucson and Mexico's special representative dealing with the *revoltosos* on the border, reported that Charles F. Stevens, a deputy United States marshal, had just arrived from San Antonio. Stevens was attached to the El Paso marshal's office "with the exclusive object of arresting Práxedis Guerrero." The main problem this time was not locating Guerrero, but making a positive identification. There was still no one in the El Paso area who could identify the revolutionary, and lawmen considered bringing in someone from Morenci who had known Guerrero. The consul—concerned about growing American opinion that was critical of the Mexican government—wrote that if Guerrero were arrested and not positively identified, "it

Arturo M. Elías, the Mexican consul in Tucson, Arizona, diligently led the unsuccessful Mexican efforts to track down and capture Guerrero. (Courtesy Arizona Historical Society/Tucson.)

would be a calamity of terrible consequences in relation to public opinion in the territory of Texas."20

Feeling the pressure, Guerrero abandoned El Paso, leaving the printing of his *chamaco*, *Punto Rojo*, in the hands of Lowe, Clemente García, and Antonio Velarde. He continued to write for the newspaper from wherever he was at the moment. The search for Práxedis intensified. In January 1910, Arturo M. Elías received an inquiry from J. Herbert Cole, special agent in charge of the investigative office of the Department of Justice in San Antonio, asking for the name and address of a person who knew Guerrero and who could identify him. Elías responded that Rubén Noveira, now with the police department in Ciudad Juárez, knew Guerrero well and could identify him. Noveira provided a minutely detailed description of Práxedis. It appeared the net was about to close on Guerrero when the Mexican consul in Galveston, Texas, alerted the United States authorities that the long-sought *revoltoso* was in Houston, meeting with another liberal conspirator, S. T. Agis.21

Guerrero was staying in the Hotel Louisiana on the street of the same name in Houston. Fred Lancaster, deputy United States marshal, a special invesigator from the Department of Justice, and Houston police planned to converge on the hotel on February 12. As it turned out only Lancaster showed up; the special agent took sick and the Houston police never appeared, apparently due to a miscommunication. According to the *Houston Chronicle*, Agis recognized Lancaster from an earlier encounter in San Antonio. When he entered the room, Guerrero exited via a third story window, jumping some thirty feet to the pavement below.22 In a letter to a sister, Práxedis described the events:

> On the 12th the henchmen of the dictatorship came to my house and I saw myself for a few moments in their hands, but taking advantage of their stupidity and cowardice I escaped through a window in my room. This is on

the third floor of the building. Tying two sheets in order to shorten the distance to the brick pavement, I hurt myself when my rope broke the moment it felt the weight of my body. The henchmen were satisfied with seizing all that they could, as is their old custom. This time they took a suitcase of yours, several newspapers, books, pamphlets, and some original articles. That was all, and they will lament it because they were expecting to find many 'compromising' documents. . . .

Don't worry about me. I am like an eagle that burnt its feathers crossing over the flames of a volcano. I feel them growing again, and I see from my retreat the space that will soon be mine. . . .[23]

The United States consular agent on special assignment regarding *insurrecto* activities for the Department of Justice, reported that, after the escape, a special agent of the Department of Justice, a deputy United States marshal, and local police were "hot on the trail," and in the opinion of the Houston police chief, capture is only a question of time. Editorializing more than a little, he wrote: " Señor P. G. Guerrero is the highest of all the many leaders of the so-called Liberal Party along the American side of the Border, and his capture has been attempted many times before, he succeeding in escaping every time. His doctrine is that the Mexicans in America have the right to arm themselves whenever and wherever they choose, and if they then desire to invade their Country and endeavor to overthrow the existing government, it is their right so to do." A week later, he had to report: "No trace of Señor Guerrero has been discovered."[24] By March the United States secretary of state described Guerrero as "a notorious revolutionist who is still at large along the border between Mexico and the United States."[25]

Guerrero was at large but his flight took him nowhere exotic. He went to the North Texas town of Bridgeport to work in the coal mines. He had to support himself and to sustain *Punto Rojo*, which was still being published in El Paso. Guerrero contributed articles to his own periodical and also to *Evolución Social*, a weekly published by León Cárdenas Martínez (a special delegate of the junta) in the far West Texas railroad center of Toyah. *Punto Rojo*, which at its peak had a circulation of 10,000 copies, was suppressed in April 1910 after criminal libel charges were brought by agents of the Mexican government. The United States government was also offering a $10,000 reward for the capture of Guerrero, still wanted on charges of violating the neutrality laws.[26] Turner commented on these events in *Barbarous Mexico*:

> Only a short time ago the news was printed that *Punto Rojo*, an anti-Díaz labor paper of Texas, had been suppressed, that $10,000 reward had been offered for the capture of its editor, Práxedis Guerrero, that secret service men in pursuit of that reward had seized subscription books of the paper and from the books had secured names of men who would be at once proceeded against.
>
> During the past three years persecution of this general character has directly caused the suspension of at least ten newspapers printed in Spanish along the border for Mexican readers.[27]

Guerrero stayed in Bridgeport, anonymous among the many Mexican miners there. In June 1910 he wrote a sister:

> Now I have been working in the coal mines which are certainly very uncomfortable, and I have not felt the pains in my waist that I had felt for a few weeks after the accident in Houston. . . .
>
> It won't be long before I again begin to cultivate my dear red flowers. You will see them more serene and proud than ever before.
>
> Keep that check for me as a 'souvenir' of the bourgeois

that exploits us here. Through it you will see the famous *'tiendas de raya'* are as popular in *Yanquilandia* as they are in México. . . .

They say the government in Washington, by their own admission, offered ten thousand dollars for the capture of Prax. It seems to me that it is not worthwhile to spend what is taken from the people, because at the end of everything they will not be able to stop the tempest. The old man, for his part, is opening the veins of the unfortunate Mexican Treasury with the purpose of stifling all that wander here. Sad blindness. There are things that you cannot kill and you cannot imprison. . . .[28]

At the end of June, Guerrero left Bridgeport to avoid capture. He traveled to several Texas cities, staying for a time in another railroad town, Derby, before returning to San Antonio. There were some pressing new reasons why the United States authorities wanted Guerrero in custody. Ricardo Flores Magón, Antonio I. Villarreal, and Librado Rivera were scheduled to be released from the territorial prison in Arizona in August 1910. Department of Justice representatives—now considering ways of keeping them locked up—were fearful they would resume their revolutionary activities as soon as they were free. There were charges of violating the neutrality law in Texas against Flores Magón and Villarreal for issuing orders for the 1908 revolts. However, the United States attorney did not feel he could get a conviction unless the actual leaders of the revolt, Práxedis Guerrero and Enrique Flores Magón, were tried at the same time.[29]

Guerrero spent most of the summer of 1910 in San Antonio. As the outbreak of the revolution approached Guerrero seemed to be thinking beyond Mexico. He gave thought to the development of a "Pan American Labor League" or an "International League of Workers." He even drew up a program and plan of organization for what he called finally the "Pan American Labor

League" and organized some followers in San Antonio.³⁰

On August 3, 1910, Flores Magón and his confederates were released from prison at Florence, Arizona. Instead of coming to Texas, from where it seemed the revolution would most likely erupt, they went to California. The restless Guerrero was eager to enter the fray, but at the same time seemed obligated to join the junta leaders in Los Angeles. Learning of the recent execution of José Lugo, the leader of the revolt in Viesca, Coahuila, in 1908, Guerrero wrote in a letter:

> The fight becomes more intense every day. For my part, I will soon abandon this land; I will go to Mexico and will experience the same luck as Lugo or I will fulfill my purpose. Nobody sends me and I go against the opinion of some comrades, who without doubt wish to see me die of boredom in this hypocrite country.³¹

Toward the end of August, Guerrero did in fact go to Los Angeles, delaying for only a short while his determination to enter Mexico in revolt. As usual his family was concerned about his safety, especially now that they knew of the reward posted for his capture. Reassuring his sister, he wrote "my sufferings are not as large as you imagine. Your love for me makes the acts larger, and thus, the one who suffers most is you. If you would see this from up close, you would see it as so simple and natural that you would not have tortuous thoughts on my account. . . ."³²

In Los Angeles, the *magonistas* began once again to publish *Regeneración*, the first issue was dated September 3, 1910. Ricardo Flores Magón was the director, with Anselmo L. Figueroa serving as editor. The editorial board included Práxedis, Antonio I. Villarreal, Librado Rivera, Enrique Flores Magón, and Lázaro Gutiérrez de Lara. An English page, edited by Los Angeles socialist Alfred G. Sanftleben, was included in this renascence of *Regeneración*. Sanftleben left the paper in December after a conflict with Ricardo over support for the developing revolutionary movement led by Francisco I. Madero in Mexico. Ethel Duffy Turner, the wife of John Kenneth Turner, took over most of the preparation of the English page.33

The Turners had been involved with the PLM to some extent ever since arriving in California in the fall of 1907. Ethel Duffy Turner remembered the fall of 1910 as an exciting time in the movement. The Riveras made their home in the same building where *Regeneración* was produced and everyone involved came together for the noon meal prepared by Concha Rivera, Librado's wife, and some of the other women. Ricardo, who with pen in hand always had plenty to say, usually listened as his more outgoing younger brother, Enrique, or the earnest young Práxedis dominated the conversations.34

Guerrero wrote for *Regeneración* from the beginning, although some of the articles had earlier appeared in *Punto Rojo*. In the first issue, his article, "Something Else," dealt with discrimination against and exploitation of Mexicans in the United States. In subsequent weeks his accounts of the battles of the 1908 revolt—Las Vacas, Viesca, and Palomas—appeared, accompanied and followed by articles on all manner of issues. Beginning with the second issue, Guerrero's *"puntos rojos"* became a feature of the new *Regeneración*. These were short commentaries, aphorisms, calls to arms, and the like, which circulated widely. The main body of the collected writings of Guerrero appeared in *Regeneración* in 1910 and, posthumously, in 1911.35

In the fall of 1910 signs of the impending revolution were more and more evident, and Guerrero knew he had to be part of it. By 1910, the movement against the Porfiriato and Francisco I. Madero's campaign for the presidency had forced many more Mexican exiles to the United States, lessening attention paid to the *magonistas*. Madero drew considerable support in both Mexico and the United States from middle- and upper-class interests advocating democratic political reform in Mexico—interests that generally shied away from, or actively opposed, the

American radicals John Kenneth and Ethel Duffy Turner were probably the only norteamericanos *befriended by Guerrero. (Author's collection.)*

social and economic reforms of the liberals. Still, as early as May there had been conflict in Tlaxcala with some *PLM* overtones, and Veracruz was about to erupt again. Cándido Donato Padua, participant and historian of the Veracruz Liberal movement, had been in contact with Guerrero while he was in San Antonio in the summer of 1910. Práxedis wrote Padua that he wanted to join the rebels in Veracruz, and when the charismatic chieftain, Santana Rodríguez, or Santanón, enlisted in the cause, he was commissioned in a document signed for the *PLM* by Ricardo Flores Magón and Guerrero.36

Meanwhile, Madero, after being arrested in the course of his election campaign against Díaz, had gained his freedom and fled to San Antonio. From there he called for a revolt to begin on November 20, 1910. Guerrero had earlier scoffed at claims that Madero represented the interests of the agrarian workers in Mexico. The *Monitor Democrático*, an anti-Díaz but not radical San Antonio newspaper, had reported that Madero was an "agricultural worker" who had "sweated at the sides of his workers." Guerrero, writing in *Punto Rojo*, recorded that Madero was not an "agricultural worker" but a great landowner; an *hacendado* who, with more or less "mercy, exploited Mexican workers." If Madero was an "agricultural worker," than so were Terrazas, Creel, and the rest. "Don't dress your idols in tissue paper," Guerrero warned, "because they usually 'sweat' in the parades." Now as responses to Madero's appeal to arms began to grow in Mexico, Guerrero saw the *PLM* in danger of being engulfed in the *maderista* movement. By the end of November there were groups of liberals fighting in Sonora, Chihuahua, Tlaxcala, Morelos, Durango, Oaxaca, Tabasco, and Veracruz. Práxedis felt compelled to join them.37

Against the wishes of Flores Magón, who wanted to keep him with *Regeneración*, Guerrero left Los Angeles at the end of November 1910. Before leaving California, he gave his books, including many works on anarchism, to Antonio Rivera, the son of Librado. Then he went by the home of the Turners, leaving most of his personal effects with Ethel Duffy Turner. "If I do not return, Ethel, send them to her [his sister in Guanajuato], and I know I will not return," Práxedis said, as he left for El Paso, Texas. Gutiérrez de Lara accompanied him.[38]

In El Paso, Guerrero could call on many veterans of the earlier efforts to topple the Díaz government. Prisciliano G. Silva had already served prison time for violating the neutrality laws and he and his son, Benjamín, were ready to try again. Several of the veterans of the 1908 attack on Las Vacas also were willing to follow Guerrero. José Inés Salazar, who had participated in the attack on Palomas, also signed up. On December 19 Guerrero led his force of twenty-two across the Río Grande near Ciudad Juárez, quickly moving south into the Chihuahua desert. About forty kilometers from Ciudad Juárez, they hijacked a train that took them to the Guzmán station. Appropriating horses, arms, and food, the *magonista* rebels prepared to march on the city of Casas Grandes. If successful at Casas Grandes, they would be ready to march on Chihuahua city. They hoped to gain recruits and support along the way.

After advancing south of Guzmán, Guerrero led his forces back to that small town to make it his headquarters. Here he divided his forces, which had grown since crossing the border, sending some under Prisciliano Silva to operate in other parts of Chihuahua. Gutiérrez de Lara went with this group, which would soon clash with Madero's forces. To distinguish themselves from the *maderista* rebels, Guerrero's men flew a red flag emblazoned with the slogan *"Tierra y Libertad."* Guerrero now commanded thirty-two well-armed and mounted troops. With these fighters he occupied Corralitos, some eighty kilometers south of Guzmán. On December 28, Guerrero boldly demanded the surrender of Casas Grandes. Although there were about 450 federal troops plus about twenty *rurales* and civil guards in the city, the *jefe político*, not knowing Guerrero's numbers, frantically wired Chihuahua for help. One hundred fifty additional troops arrived the next day.

Realizing he could not take Casas Grandes with the forces at hand, Guerrero led his troops northwest on December 29 toward Janos, where he hoped to obtain supplies and recruits. The *presidente municipal* of Janos, though he had about as many troops at his disposal as the liberals, said he would surrender the town to them on the morning of December 30. Meanwhile, he wired Casas Grandes for help. When Guerrero learned of this action, he led an assault on Janos, commencing about 10 P.M. the night of the twenty-ninth. After intense fighting the rebels gained control of the town. No sooner did the victory seem secure than the troops from Casas Grandes arrived and heavy fighting ensued. In the battle, Guerrero took to a roof top and was mortally wounded in the head. The loss of their leader seemed to inspire his troops as they drove the federal forces from the town. In the end, however, the liberals had to give up the town, leaving Guerrero's body behind.[39]

The news from Janos was a bitter blow for the junta leaders in Los Angeles. Ricardo Flores Magón wrote of the loss in the pages of *Regeneración*, dated January 11, 1911:

> . . . on the glorious day of Janos Práxedis G. Guerrero, the young fighter for liberty gave up his life. . . .
>
> Práxedis was the soul of the movement for freedom. Unhesitatingly it can be said that Práxedis was one of the purest, worthiest, most intelligent, self-denying and bravest men that ever espoused the cause of the disinherited, and the vacancy caused by his departure can never be filled. Where can a man be found so free from personal ambitions of any kind, all brain and heart, brave and active as he was?
> . . .
> Without exaggeration it may be said that it is not Mexico that has lost one of her best sons, but that it was all humanity, for Práxedis was a fighter for the freedom of all. . . .[40]

John Kenneth Turner also reported in *Regeneración*:

The price of despotism in a given country is the blood of her best and bravest sons. Of the thousands of good and brave men whom Porfirio Díaz has killed in order to perpetuate his personal rule over Mexico, I cannot believe that any was better or braver than Práxedis Guerrero.[41]

PART II
THE WRITER AND HIS MILIEU

FRIENDS AND FOES: THE WORLD OF THE MEXICAN IN THE UNITED STATES

Práxedis Guerrero, born in Mexico and died in Mexico, spent almost all the last six years of his life in the United States. In that time he progressed from a lowly laborer in developing American industries to a leader in a major revolutionary movement working to overthrow the government of Porfirio Díaz. Living and working throughout the American Southwest, Guerrero made many new acquaintances—friends as well as enemies—and his relationships in the United States—with both men and women—were important to his intellectual development. Despite his strong belief in Mexican nationalism, he, like many *revoltosos*, was something of a dreamer, which took him beyond national boundaries. He had grown in political and ideological maturity, and, it can be said, he considered himself a citizen of the world. His experiences, however, were those of what present-day generations call "Mexican American." Out of this setting emerges a more complete picture of Guerrero and the events along the United States-Mexican borderlands in the years before the Mexican Revolution that would shape him.

As best can be determined, Guerrero did not have any contacts in the United States before his arrival in the fall of 1904. He did not come alone, of course, bringing childhood friend, Francisco Manrique, and another Guanajauto acquaintance, Manuel Vázquez. Confident and capable, he apparently never had problems securing employment. Within five months of his arrival, he began *Alba Roja* in San Franciso, using it as a vehicle to publicize and confront issues facing laborers in the United States. Later, when he moved to Morenci, Arizona, he quickly took a leading role in organizing the workers. Of course, Guerrero and Manrique were both educated young men from landed families in Mexico, putting them in a rather unusual position among other Mexican workers in the borderlands—workers who were generally uneducated immigrants driven to the United States by economic need.[1]

In Morenci Guerrero first made contact with Manuel Sarabia, *Partido Liberal Mexicano* junta member and journalist. It was the beginning of a close and lasting friendship, albeit one that would have to survive some political and personal differences along the way. Sarabia may have come to Morenci in May 1906 as part of the PLM effort to help insure wide reception of the forthcoming *Programa y Manifesto*, which would herald the hoped-for revolt of 1906. Although it was not a border town, there were a great number of Mexicans working in the mines in and around Morenci and nearby Clifton, Arizona. Shortly after the meetings with Sarabia, Guerrero organized the *Obreros Libres*, the workers' organization that affiliated with the PLM. While Guerrero stayed in Morenci, Sarabia went to Chicago, where, using the alias Sam Moret, he worked on a newspaper. Neither Práxedis nor Sarabia played any direct role in the attempted revolt of 1906, even though Sarabia, as a junta member, would later be held responsible for some of the *PLM* involvement.²

The disastrous results of the 1906 insurrection brought Guerrero and Sarabia together again. Manuel's cousin, junta Vice-President Juan Sarabia, was arrested and imprisoned in Mexico. Ricardo Flores Magón and most of the other *PLM* leaders were in hiding, evading arrest for violating neutrality laws. In June 1907, Flores Magón established *Revolución* in Los Angeles. Práxedis moved to the border town of Douglas, Arizona, about the same time and started contributing articles to *Revolución*. Sarabia came to Douglas to work on a local newspaper, sharing living quarters with Guerrero. The hows and whys all this came about are not clear except that Guerrero and Sarabia were drawing closer and that Práxides would contribute more and more to the liberal movement. And the stage for these players would change quickly.

Only a month after his arrival in Douglas, Sarabia was kidnapped, becoming a *cause celèbre* in the United States. Práxedis wrote extensively, then and later, about the event, bringing him more into the *PLM* limelight. In October 1907, following the arrests of Flores Magón and the other junta leaders, Sarabia and Guerrero left Douglas for Los Angeles to take over direction of *Revolución*. They worked together in California until January when Sarabia was arrested on the same charges that Flores Magón, Antonio Villarreal, and Librado Rivera were fighting. Sarabia did not fight extradition and was taken to Arizona in May 1908. Guerrero remained in Los Angeles, trying to keep *Revolución* in print. Sarabia would not go to court right away; United States attorneys wanted to try Flores Magón first. At the end of October 1908, a new player would enter the scene: Elizabeth Darling Trowbridge, a Boston heiress who had attached herself to the liberal cause, put up bail money to free Sarabia, bondable because government attorneys considered him "nothing but a tool" of Flores Magón. Less than two months later Sarabia and Trowbridge were married. In early 1909, forfeiting the bond, the couple fled to England.³

Thus, the junta member who brought Guerrero into the movement, abandoned him. They had been together about six months, which, except for Manrique, was a long association for the peripatetic Práxedis. It was over a year before Guerrero communicated with Sarabia, responding finally to a letter from England, greeting him as "My dear friend":

> I received your letter, but I did not answer it because I believed you were a bourgeois; you married a person considered rich; and your distance from me made me think in such a manner. Today I know this is not true, and that distance and all, you still try to fight the common enemy. So I break my silence and talk to you with my customary rude frankness.

After some talk of tactics and the difference between the radical struggles in Europe and America, Guerrero wrote, "I don't believe that things are right for your return. If sometime you return, let it not be in order to surrender, but in order to fight."[4]

With the ice broken, other letters followed. On June 16, 1910, Práxedis told Manuel he was developing a plan to free Sarabia's cousin Juan from prison in Mexico. "In general one should have very little faith in lawyers; it is better to accelerate revolutionary justice than to request it from the tyrant's hand," he wrote. Nearing the second anniversry of the death of Manrique, he remembered: "The bullets of the tyranny have prematurely snatched our partner, who would have been an immense hero." Such a remembrance brought the following thoughts: "Yes, one feels the nostalgia for the friendship, one feels sorrow at the absence of those who broke with us the bread of the idea and the fatigues of the rough pilgrimage. On the beach, or fighting with the threatening surf, there always remains in the mind an unbreakable thread that ties us to the memory."

Guerrero was in Bridgeport, Texas, when he wrote the above, explaining, "I am working in the coal mines to get some money. This means I have very few free moments, or rather none."[5] About a month and one half later, he again wrote to Sarabia, "I have had the intention of answering your more recent letters . . . but the demands of my vagabond life [impose their] tyranny on me." By this time, August of 1910, Práxedis was steeling himself to enter the armed revolt once again—writing about it was not enough. "I believe that you will agree with me that the word is an excellent medium, whose efficacy is well known, but it should not become the 'chronic weapon for demolishing tyranny.' The revolutionary phrase, when not accompanied by deeds, or followed by them, acquires the insensitive soporific monotony of Christian prayers." Remembering 1908, he continued:

"We saw a good probability of success, and we called our companions to the fight. We went with them; treason and cowardice cut our wings upon beginning the flight and we fell, only to lift ourselves up to continue the fight, calling for death or victory for those who want to follow us, be it few or many." Guerrero looked to the future fight with a certain grimness, writing Sarabia, ". . . the persecution, and the fight with its multiple accidents has changed me somewhat since you met me. Now, I neither love nor hate, the strength of feeling has gone to the conscience. The live ember that sparked the forge is now the tool that coldly executes its mission."[6]

In one of his last letters to Manuel, written from San Antonio shortly before going to Los Angeles to join the newly freed Ricardo Flores Magón, Guerrero reminisced about how Sarabia had been instrumental in bringing him into the movement, ". . . so that I would dedicate all my energies to the work of the cause. The events that occurred later put me in a position that I would have rejected one hundred times if things had gone easily and comfortably. For a long time I have been an enemy of tyrants, but I have always had a large dose of skepticism in my brain." Before he had joined the movement, he wrote Manuel, he had needed to study it carefully, ". . . until I understood your sincerity, until I saw you closely and knew that my efforts were necessary. Without your visit to Morenci, without the subsequent events: your kidnapping, the imprisonment of the comrades in Los Angeles, and the difficulties that constantly plagued us, my inadequacies would not have seen me obligated to take a superior role."7

Guerrero's relations with the Flores Magón brothers were more complex. Enrique Flores Magón arrived in Los Angeles shortly after Guerrero and Sarabia moved there from Douglas in October 1907. They worked together on *Revolución*. In November, Práxedis went to the Los Angeles County jail for his first face-to-face meeting with Ricardo Flores Magón, Antonio I. Villarreal, and Librado Rivera. He must have impressed them because within a few weeks he was designated second secretary of the *PLM* junta. Although Guerrero remained in Los Angeles until the end of May 1908, it is not known if he visited Ricardo often. It is doubtful, for there were people closer to Flores Magón who tried to visit him but were unsuccessful. Part of the time the Mexican *revoltosos* were held incommunicado. Práxedis did receive considerable correspondence from Ricardo, particularly when they were trying to start another newspaper after *Revolución* was suppressed early in 1908.

Through these months Práxedis and Enrique obviously spent a great deal of time together. They were able to revive *Revolución* briefly in April and May 1908. After the final suppression of the paper Guerrero, accompanied by Manrique, went to El Paso to begin preparations for the expected revolt in the summer of 1908. Enrique followed soon after. Several letters during the period reveal relations among these revolutionary leaders. Because all of Ricardo's comunications from the county jail were intercepted, the letters detailing plans for the uprising contributed to the failures of 1908. One letter in particular, to Enrique, not only revealed aspects of plans for the revolt but scathingly criticized the United States citizenry for not being concerned about the plight of the downtrodden. Another letter, addressed to both Enrique and Práxedis, explained at length the anarchist elements in the coming revolt.[8]

Before joining Práxedis in El Paso, Enrique wrote a letter advising him not to go into Mexico. This is of interest because Enrique did not participate in the attack on Palomas. He "accidentally" wounded himself before Guerrero led the *revoltosos* across the Río

Grande. Guerrero knew it was no accident, but in later years, after most of the principals were dead, Enrique claimed in detailed accounts to have taken part in the campaign. Some assert this created a rift between Guerrero and the Flores Magóns, but nothing substantiates such a claim. Although Guerrero blamed the failures of 1908 on treachery and cowardice, there is no indication he referred to Enrique. Moreover, Práxedis and Ricardo were both dead before Enrique made his statements.[9]

After the failure at Palomas, which cost Guerrero his closest friend, Manrique, Práxedis went to Albuquerque, New Mexico, joining Enrique there as both were recovering from their wounds. Enrique left soon to find work in San Francisco and Práxedis went back to Douglas, Arizona. Later, early in 1909, Guerrero made a special trip to San Francisco to inform Enrique of revolutionary plans. Even though proclamations and manifestos were issued over the signatures of Práxedis and Enrique, the two spent little time together until the fall of 1910.[10] From late August 1910, when he went to Los Angeles, until the end of November 1910, when he began his fatal campaign, Guerrero worked with both Flores Magóns in producing *Regeneración* and in trying once again to prepare for the revolution. This three-month period is the only time that Práxedis and Ricardo were together, a short time given the feelings of respect and admiration they developed for one another.

Roaming the borderlands from California to Texas in 1909 and 1910, Guerrero came to know practically all of the leading *PLM* supporters. He maintained an extensive correspondence with the *magonistas*, most of it dealing with bread-and-butter issues—how to raise money, from whom to buy arms and ammunition, where to send the newspapers to be distributed to various subscribers. He also gained confidence as the time passed. In a 1909 letter to Manuel's brother, for example, Tomás Sarabia, who had been one of the principal organizers in Texas for years, Guerrero wrote, "Instructions in these moments are reduced to one word only—Work." Prisciliano Silva in El Paso, Jesús María Rangel in San Antonio, and other seasoned veterans of the struggle recognized Guerrero's leadership. In his final campaign in 1910, Silva followed him as did Lázaro Gutiérrez de Lara, the lawyer-journalist already recognized as one of the principal Mexican opposition spokesmen in the United States.[11]

Besides his demonstrated abilities as a writer, another factor that gave Guerrero credibility was his military experience. His time with the Second Military Reserve in Guanajuato gave him military skills, or, at least more knowledge than other *magonistas* had. While his education and his writings made him welcome in homes such as that of the long-time El Paso publisher Lauro Aguirre, his willingness to work at manual labor to support himself gained the confidence of workers. His relative youth was not a factor. He was the same age as Juan Sarabia and in the same general age group as Manuel and Tomás Sarabia. He was a year older than Antonio de P. Araujo. Villarreal was three years older, Enrique five, and Ricardo only eight years older. For the most part, the *magonistas* were not old men.

Further, the *magonistas* were not all men. Guerrero's attitudes about and relationships with women are important to an understanding of his career. His letters home indicate the strong feelings Práxedis had for his mother, although she could not dissuade him from his commitment to radical activism. His sisters, too, remained close. He shared his feelings on many issues in his letters to them. He was as comfortable around women as he was around men and perhaps growing up with several sisters contributed to that ease. On the other hand, any intimate relationships with women remain a mystery. In July 1908, the Mexican consul in Tucson, trying to obtain a photo with which to identify Guerrero, reported contacting a young woman in Morenci with whom Práxedis "had relations." This is the only such reference and certainly nothing on which to construct a sexual history. What is certain is that Guerrero's constant movement from 1908 on, his need to support himself and his devotion to the cause left little time for social life.[12]

There were women within the *magonista* movement from the very beginning. When Ricardo Flores Magón crossed into the

United States at Laredo, Texas, in 1904, Sara Estela Ramírez, editor of an exile paper, *La Corregidora*, gave assistance. By the time the liberal leaders moved their base of operations to St. Louis early in 1905, the movement resembled an extended family. Librado Rivera, one of the elders of the group, brought his wife and children with him when he came from San Luis Potosí. Juan Sarabia, from the same state, was accompanied by his mother. The move to St. Louis had been instigated by Antonio I. Villarreal, a former student of Rivera's, who was from Lampazos, Nuevo León. From that northern frontier town would come Villarreal's father, Próspero, a brother of the same name, and his two sisters Andrea and Teresa.[13]

The Villarreal González sisters (in particular Andrea) became the best known of the female Mexican exiles. Andrea was linked romantically with Juan Sarabia and later with Aaron López Manzano, the printer-compositor on *Regeneración*, who was arrested with Librado Rivera in 1906. At the time Rivera was the last junta member still in St. Louis and he left shortly after the incident. The families, however, stayed in Missouri for some time. Rivera's family moved to California after Rivera was arrested with Flores Magón and Villarreal. The Villarreal sisters moved to San Antonio in late summer 1908. Even though the junta leadership had all left the city, St. Louis was still considered the home of the *PLM*.

St. Louis newspapers—much to the chagrin of the Mexican government and its representatives—were most active in following the activities of the *magonistas*.[14] Reporters relished having an attractive young woman such as Andrea as a spokesperson for what was depicted as a somewhat romantic revolutionary movement. A Sunday article in the *St. Louis Post-Dispatch* in December 1906, titled "The Thrilling History of the St. Louis Junta," for example, featured Andrea along with all the members of the junta. The Mexican consul in St. Louis reported that the Villarreal sisters, "well known in this city," were often quoted in the local press, "making them appear as heroines persecuted by the Mexican government, without doubt in order to obtain material for sensational stories."[15] Andrea, besides representing the *PLM* to the press, fancied

The Villarreal González sisters, Teresa and Andrea, drew international attention for their revolutionary efforts. The image was reproduced from the St. Louis Post-Dispatch, for November 22, 1906, which featured a front-page article about the women.

herself a writer and began to contribute to oppsition papers such as *El Progreso* in San Antonio. Even though Manuel Sarabia characterized some of her work as "terrible" in 1907, his brother, Tomás, asked Andrea to write for *Reforma, Libertad, y Justicia*, the paper he and Antonio de P. Araujo started in 1908. She contributed articles, concluding one with words she attributed to Karl Marx: "Give me liberty or give me death."[16]

On the other hand, she could be a fiery defender of the cause. After the 1908 attacks on Viesca, Las Vacas, and Palomas, *The New York Times* interviewed Andrea in St. Louis, describing her as a "poetess, and one of the leading spirits of the Mexican junta." She told the *Times* that "the real revolution will envelope Mexico in a whirlwind." Defending the rebels' theft of money from the bank in Viesca, she asked, "Where else would the revolutionists get money for ammunition and guns with which to win liberty and to buy food for themselves and their wives and children?" She concluded, "I am a woman, and I hate bloodshed and violence. But if it became necessary I could myself use the dagger or the torch."[17]

Práxedis Guerrero apparently made his first contacts with the Villarreal sisters after the move to San Antonio. By that time, Guerrero was on the go constantly. He was also assuming more and more leadership responsibilities, so frequent communications and meetings would be inevitable. In 1909 the Villarreals went to Arizona for the trial of their brother Antonio on neutrality law violations. When he was convicted with Ricardo Flores Magón and Rivera, the sisters stayed in Arizona for a time, living in Phoenix. As was often the case, however, money was short and it was difficult to make ends meet in the area. At the same time it was hard to move.[18]

Later in 1909, after the convictions of the liberal leaders, the Villarreal sisters returned to Texas as advocates for the *PLM* against Díaz. By this time Andrea had become so well known that even the Mexican consul in Del Rio referred to her as the "Mexican Joan of Arc," a rather extravagant label first used by a San Antonio newpaper reporter.[19] In San Antonio both women quickly became involved in publishing ventures. Andrea was identified with *Mujer*

Moderna and Teresa edited *El Obrero*. Their involvement in these papers raises some intriguing questions. In 1907 in El Paso, *La Voz de la Mujer* advocated the cause of the *magonistas* on behalf of women. Isidra T. de Cárdenas was the director; the staff was composed of women, except for the secretary of the editorial board, who was Isidra's husband, León Cárdenas. Cárdenas was a delegate of the PLM junta and in August 1907 he wrote a revealing letter to junta member Antonio I. Villarreal. He said he had added his name to the masthead as secretary because Lauro Aguirre, the well-known El Paso publisher, feared people would think he was writing the articles in *La Voz de la Mujer*. In fact, Cárdenas wrote, he *was* writing the articles because "the ladies who appear as the editors only have a big heart for the cause but cannot express themselves because they are incapable of writing." He did so in part, he went on to say, to gain support for movement.[20]

Were the Villarreal sisters editing the San Antonio newspapers or simply fronting for manipulative male *insurrectos*? Andrea Villarreal wrote and spoke often on a variety of issues, and she may have written much of what appeared in *Mujer Moderna*. Teresa tended to be less vocal. It is known, since a United States government informant gained the confidence of both women in San Antonio, that Guerrero had considerable contact with them in the spring and summmer of 1910. He published several pieces in *El Obrero* using the name "Victoria Segura"; some of the essays were later reprinted in the revived *Regeneración* under his own name.[21]

Guerrero addressed the theme of women in the struggle in several of his writings. In "Revolutionary Women," originally published in *Punto Rojo*, he echoed some of the themes that Cárdenas had mentioned in his letter to Villarreal. He wrote, "When a woman fights, what man, no matter how miserable and fainthearted he may be, can turn his back, without blushing? Revolutionary Women: the day you see us hesitate, please spit in our faces!"[22] Given such views, one may well imagine Guerrero supporting a prominent role for women to "shame" men into supporting the *magonista* cause. In a longer article titled "Women," he made clear his support for the libertarian view of equality of men and women. He rejected, however, the "digression known as feminism." Writing further on what he called the "emancipation of women," he concluded:

> Freedom scares those who do not understand it and those who have created their environments from the degradation and misery of other people; and that is why the emancipation of women finds a hundred opponents for every man who defends or works for women.
>
> Libertarian equality does not attempt to turn a woman into a *man*; it gives the same opportunities to both factions of the human species, so that both can develop without obstacles, naturally benefiting from the mutual support, without snatching away each other's rights, without obstructing the place that each of them has in nature. We men and women must fight for that rational equality, the harmonizer of the individual happiness with the collective happiness, because without it, there will perpetually exist in the homes, a seed of tyranny, which is the sprout of slavery and social misfortune. If customs are a yoke, let us break the customs, however sacred they may seem; by offending customs civilization advances. Customs may be a restraint, but restraints have never liberated people, satisfied hunger, nor redeemed slavery.[23]

Clearly believing the roles of men and women were well defined, Guerrero wrote in one of his later "Puntos Rojos" essays published in *Regeneración*: "To the repugnant spectacle of the policewoman, they give the name feminism; this deplorable mannishness being the opposite of the idea this modern word expresses." Yet, of the six goals in the program of his "Pan American Labor League," a hoped-for organization of workers of both sexes in all the Americas, Guerrero listed as number two: "emancipation of women." Emancipation, yes, but his message was essentially that men were men and women were women.[24]

Guerrero had fewer contacts with the women of the cause in

California. When Ricardo Flores Magón, Villarreal, and Rivera were arrested in Los Angeles in August 1907 the resulting publicity brought new adherents. Ethel Mowbray Dolson, who first visited the liberals in the Los Angeles County jail as a journalist, became a messenger for the junta leaders. Shortly after the *revoltosos'* arrests, Ethel Duffy and John Kenneth Turner moved to Los Angeles, learned of the Mexicans from socialist contacts and became involved. It was after interviewing Flores Magón in jail that Turner went to Mexico to see for himself if the evils of the Porfiriato were as alleged by the *magonistas*. This was the trip that resulted in *Barbarous Mexico*.

Early in 1908, Elizabeth Darling Trowbridge, a Boston heiress with libertarian leanings, arrived in Los Angeles, joined the group, and became a close friend of Ethel Duffy Turner. Trowbridge also became a source of financial support for the liberal cause, assisting in defense costs, as well as providing help with the living expenses of Librado Rivera's wife and children and the family Ricardo had acquired, his companion María Brousse Talavera and her daughter Lucía Norman. Ethel Duffy Turner remembered this as a time of excitement as the young women got caught up in the movement. Although Práxedis was in Los Angeles working on *Revolución* and trying to start other papers (after *Revolución* was suppressed) part of the time, he probably did not have a lot of contact with this new group of partisans. Moreover, he would soon be involved in the revolts of 1908.

In the summer and fall of 1908, while Guerrero was fighting his battles and licking his wounds, the Los Angeles supporters moved to Tucson near where the *magonistas* would be taken for trial. John Murray, a socialist who had also gone to Mexico on a Trowbridge-financed investigative trip, led the move to Arizona. Trowbridge and Ethel Duffy Turner followed him there and John Kenneth Turner joined them on his return from Mexico. In Arizona they started a magazine titled *The Border*, which took up the Liberals' cause. After Trowbridge helped Manuel Sarabia get out of jail on bail, Sarabia tried to start *El Defensor del Pueblo*. Trowbridge, meanwhile, published pamphlets about the "political prisoners" being held in the United States. The flurry of activity rapidly drew to a close at the end of the year, however. Murray left to work for the Chicago-based Political Refugee Defense League. The Turners went to New York to sell John's articles on Mexico. The offices of *El Defensor del Pueblo* were looted, and, shortly thereafter, Sarabia and Trowbridge married and left for England.25

Guerrero, of course, reestablished contact with Sarabia later, and came to be very close to the Turners in the last months of his life. In those last months in Los Angeles in the fall of 1910 Práxedis was in close contact with Ethel Duffy Turner, both of them working on the weekly publication of *Regeneración*. Also, by this time Guerrero had been directing the movement for over two years and certainly must have been more confident. Still, entrusting his personal belongings for his family to a foreigner as he did before he left for his fatal venture into Mexico revealed a depth of friendship rare for the reserved Guerrero. Further, the experiences of the Liberals in the United States had given all of them ample reason to be suspicious of *norteamericanos*.

Práxedis spent his last six years in the United States, almost totally in the southwestern border states where ethnic and racial discrimination against Mexicans, and Mexican Americans, was strong. For example, a United States marshal wrote in a report that the "Mexican people living on our borders are treacherous, clandestine and secretive." Luther Ellsworth, agent for the United States in border activities concerning the *revoltosos*, wrote often about "Bad Mexicans" or "the 'bad' counties" in Texas.26 Most of the liberals came with few resources and faced further economic discrimination. The junta leadership, if not evading arrest or fighting legal battles, spent most of the time editing and publishing periodicals. Obtaining the dollars to support such activities was a constant struggle. Guerrero worked to support himself and his causes, but like the others, often found himself in difficult economic conditions.

Working in the mines in Morenci, Arizona, Guerrero referred to his "humble" room. In 1906, after the junta leaders had left St.

Luther Ellsworth, American consul at Ciudad Porfirio Díaz (now Piedras Negras), Coahuila, enthusiastically took on the responsibility of hunting down revoltosos. Guerrero eluded him.

Louis, a newspaper reporter found the Villarreal sisters and father, Rivera's family, Juan Sarabia's mother and a few others living in quarters he described as: "The surroundings are dismal and in the rooms are evidence of poverty of the most pinching sort." Still, the United States offered them hope, as one of the sisters said, "No, we will not go back to Mexico. This is a free country. One can live here, though it is cold—not like our Mexico—but free."[27] Almost two years later, when a *New York Times* reporter interviewed Andrea, she was characterized as "living in the attic of a ramshackle brick building at 1014 North Tenth Street, a neighborhood populated with negroes...."[28]

Many times the correspondence of the *revoltosos* contained comments about the difficulties brought on by the shortage of funds, but never was it ever expressed as a personal complaint. Guerrero once referred to San Antonio as "Hungryopolis," but he, as well as the others, knew that their economic deprivation was a matter of choice. The dedication and level of commitment remained remarkably high throughout the struggle to overthrow the Porfiriato. On the other hand, after failures at revolt and as increasing difficulties with the authorities in the United States developed, their attitudes toward the United States began to sour. First, their hostility was directed against the government as an ally of Díaz, and later, as they ran into more and more racism and discrimination, against many of the *norteamericanos*.

The kidnapping of Manuel Sarabia, with the obvious collusion of local authorities in Arizona, bothered Guerrero immensely. He wrote about it many times. As he was hunted across the borderlands he became much more aware of the cooperation of the two nations in running down the *magonistas*. He documented cases of "persecutions and kidnappings" since 1906 in a proclamation he wrote in late 1909, describing some of the "innumerable cases of arrests, kidnappings, and clandestine deportations . . . in the last three years." One conspiracy in El Paso in October 1909 involved secret service agents from the United States Department of Justice, El Paso lawmen, Ciudad Juárez police, and private detectives whom Guerrero incorrectly identified as "Pinkertons." Guerrero described one incident:

> One night twenty men armed with revolvers, surrounded a house in El Paso, Texas, where they supposed that there were Liberals. Eight of them penetrated the interior, encountering therein only a woman and a child, who they insulted and frightened, that they might reveal what they did not know.
> Scenes like that we have just referred to have been frequent, to dishonor the hours of the night or the clear light of the day.
> The 18th of the month of October, the police of the city of Mexico, and of the city of Juárez, Mexico, together with the Federal American agents, invaded for the seventh time, the house of Señora Silva, whose husband [Prisciliano] is serving a sentence in the prison of Leavenworth, Kansas, for supposed violation of the neutrality laws. They were hunting me, and disgusted because they did not find me, they menaced as is their custom, and arrested without cause, a man who was in the house. . . .

A neighbor woman, a Spaniard, was ". . . with violence hauled by one arm to the street," where the agent, ". . . putting a pistol against her breast, interrogated her brutally."

> The Neutrality Laws are used as a pretext to haul us to American prisons, but they have not been obstacles to Mexican police, assisted by the Secret Service Agents of the United States and the Pinkerton Agency, engaging in the most scandalous and shameless behavior possible in Mexican homes on this side of the boundary line.[29]

Ricardo Flores Magón, increasingly frustrated with his court battles and not getting the support he expected from groups in the United States lashed out in a 1908 letter to Enrique:

The *norteamericanos* are incapable of feeling enthusiasm or indignation. This is truly a country of pigs. Look at the socialists: they cowardly break up in their campaign for free speech. Look at the resplendent American Federation of Labor with its million and a half members which cannot prevent the declaration of judicial 'injunctions'. . . . If the *norteamericanos* do not agitate against their own domestic miseries can we hope they will concern themselves with ours?[30]

Flores Magón's vitriolic letter was intercepted (as were all his communications) from the Los Angeles County jail, and Mexican government officials anticipated its release to the American press. Would it not backfire against the liberals? The passage was published widely, but by 1908 many Americans were questioning the country's support for Porfirio Díaz.

In the fall of 1910, Guerrero, now having spent six years north of the Río Grande, saw a connection between the plight of the Mexican American in the United States with the continuation of the Porfiriato in Mexico. In the first issue of *Regeneración* published in Los Angeles in September 1910, he addressed this matter. Pointing out that most Mexicans in the United States had emigrated to improve their economic situation, he noted that their status had actually deteriorated: it was not only the exclusion of Mexican children from the "white" schools; it was not only the "No Mexican Allowed" signs which insulted Mexicans in some stores and public places in Texas; it was not only the "Mexican Keep Away" that kept *mexicanos* living on the edges of many borderlands towns; it was not only the violent insults of the racist crowds and the abusive police drunk with the savage spirit of a lynch mob; but now even the economic promise of the United States was disappearing for Mexican immigrants. Guerrero went on to recount specific examples from Texas, Oklahoma, and Arizona to demonstrate how the situation had worsened for Mexicans in the United States. "The misery, the hunger, and the outrage are in Mexico," he wrote, but the "shame, the humiliation, and the hunger are here." The Mexicans in the

United States were caught between "two hungers," Práxedis wrote, and implicit in his writing was the call to rise against injustices on both sides of the border.[31]

Shortly before he left for that final campaign in Mexico, Práxedis learned of the actions of a lynch mob in Rocksprings, Texas, in early November 1910. It must have challenged every sense of right he had. He wrote in *Regeneración*, in an article entitled "Whites, Whites":

> A man was burned alive.
> Where?
> In the model nation, in the land of freedom, in the home of the brave, in the piece of land that still has not come out of the shadow projected by the hanging of John Brown: in the United States, in a town in Texas, called Rock Springs [sic].
> When?
> Today, in the tenth year of the century. In the age of airplanes and dirigible airships, of the wireless telegraph, of the wonderful rotary press, of the congresses of peace, of the humanitarian and animal societies.
> Who?
> A crowd of white *men*, to quote the name they prefer; white, white, white *men*.
> The people who burned this man alive were not a horde of cannibals, they were not blacks from Equatorial Africa, they were not savages from Malaysia, they were not Spanish Inquisitors, they were not red-skinned Apaches, nor Abyssinians, they were not Scythian barbarians, nor troglodytes, nor illiterate and naked inhabitants of the jungles. They were the descendants of Washington, of Lincoln, of Franklin; it was a well-dressed crowd, educated, proud of their virtues, civilized; they were the citizens and white *men* of the United States.
> Progress, civilization, culture, humanitarianism. A lie turned into an ember with the bones of Antonio Rodríguez. Dead fantasies of asphyxia, in the fetid smoke of the stake in Rock Springs.

There are schools in every town and every settlement of Texas; those schools were attended, when they were children, by the *men* of the lynch mob, their intellect was shaped in those schools; they graduated from them, to push smoldering brands into the flesh of a live man, only to say a few days after the transgression that they had done the right thing, that they acted with justice.

Schools that educate men to launch them beyond the point where the beasts are.[32]

Little wonder Práxedis Guerrero went toward his destiny in Janos with an air of fatalism.

"GLI ANARCHICI NELLA RIVOLUZIONE MESSICANA"

The ideology underlying the *Partido Liberal Mexicano* in its campaign against the dictatorship of Porfirio Díaz in Mexico has become a subject of considerable debate among those who have studied the movement. Ricardo Flores Magón, recognized today as a leading figure in the history of international anarchism, revealed his radical leanings somewhat belatedly as the movement developed. Partly this was a matter of tactics. He did not wish to alienate potential, but less radical, supporters. Evidence also shows that Flores Magón's intellectual development evolved as he struggled to foment revolution in Mexico. Práxedis Guerrero, though given to writing and speaking with "rude frankness," openly espoused anarchism while accepting the tactical necessity of supporting the *PLM*. In contrast to Flores Magón, however, he always seemed tolerant and accepting of those who differed with him. Guerrero, too, received international recognition for his commitment to anarchism.[1]

As a theory, anarchism developed between the French and Russian revolutions. It flourished as an international movement in the latter years of the nineteenth century and early years of the twentieth when the effects of industrialization weighed most heavily on workers and transformed traditional rural societies in many areas of the world. In the flowery prose of George Woodcock: "Anarchism has thrived best in lands of the sun, where it is easy to dream of golden ages of ease and simplicity, yet where the clear light also heightens the shadows of existing misery."[2]

Although anarchist beginnings are sometimes traced to ancient times, most origins of the movement are found in the eighteenth century—origins in the sense that social philosophers, with their belief in reason, progress, and human perfectability, provided the foundation for modern anarchism. Jean-Jacques Rousseau, in particular, contributed to the climate for the rise of anarchist thought in several ways. His ideas of a bucolic primitive life, the "noble savage," and, above all, the concept inherent in his "Man was born free and is everywhere in chains," are key ideas for the anarchists. Rousseau can be described as the father of numerous other movements as well, but not all his political theories were anarchistic. The development of anarchist thought came primarily from four writers or activists (named in chronological order): Englishman William Godwin, Frenchman Pierre-Joseph Proudhon, and Russians Mikhail Bakunin and Pyotr Kropotkin. The writings of Kropotkin had the most influence on Guerrero, although the latter was also much influenced by another Russian, Leo Tolstoy, and by several Spaniards, including Fernando Tarrida de Mármol and Francisco Ferrer y Guardia.

Godwin, who came out of a Calvinist tradition, achieved some fame as a novelist, but his most significant work was *Enquiry Concerning Political Justice*, published in 1793. In it, he touched on most of the ideas essential to anarchism. While he sympathized with the French Revolution, underway at the time, he saw no more hope for reforms coming from government in France than he did in England. He concluded that all government was bad. Human character, he believed, was shaped totally by environment, implying the idea of perfectability given an Edenic environment. To Godwin, education was the key in that with the right ideas, the natural equality of humankind at birth—equality in individual rights—would be preserved in a society where justice prevails. Government works against this in creating injustices by protecting the property rights of individuals. In eliminating government and property rights, which necessitate governing, one would create a society of individuals living in simple harmony.

While many of Godwin's ideas were not widely known to anarchists until late in the nineteenth century, Pierre-Joseph Proudhon attracted a broad following in his lifetime. Seeing himself in many respects as the product of the French Revolution, Proudhon was born into a modest rural family in southern France. The simple lifestyle of his early years was in sharp contrast to the harsh life of workers in the emerging industrial society of mid-nineteenth century France. In 1840 Proudhon published a pamphlet entitled *What is Property?*, and the answer he gave, "Property is theft," while an oversimplification of his views, helped establish him as the premier anarchist of his era. He was the first to call himself an anarchist and to argue that the laws by which society functions stem from the nature of society itself, not from authority. Order, he believed, comes from anarchy.

In Proudhon's view of society, work was both a social necessity and a moral virtue. The need to protect the dignity of labor from the dehumanization and exploitation of the capitalist system became a central idea in anarchist thought. He would provide this protection through the creation of voluntary communes and cooperatives where workers in small groups would coooperate in their daily economic and social life, living in a system of mutual respect for each other's individualism. Private property, in stimulating the rise of capitalism, threatened this individualism, and the state supported the capitalist system. Proudhon argued for social and economic reforms—the creation of mutual aid communes—to protect the individual, which would be followed by political reforms to eliminate the state.

Proudhon attracted wide readership and a number of followers, although he disavowed any claim of wishing to lead any kind of movement. His ideas had wide appeal to French intellectuals who reacted against the negative aspects of industrialization and the accompanying urbanization in nineteenth-century France. The egalitarian life of the village and farm society had great appeal, and Proudhon's writings of the 1840s and 1850s encouraged something of a romanticization of a peasant lifestyle. After the revolution of 1848 in France, however, and with increasing discontent among industrial workers in the 1860s, Proudhon, in the last years of his life, gave more attention to laborers. His ideas of cooperation and decentralization were advocated by many of the French workers in the founding of the First International Workingmen's Association in 1864. Proudhon may be considered a founder of anarchism, but not of the anarchist movement. In the First International, the ideological and intensely personal clash between Karl Marx and Mikhail Bakunin, a follower of Proudhon, would split the working-class movement and give rise to international anarchism.

Both Godwin and Proudhon believed that the elimination of government could be achieved without revolution, but through education and ecomomic reform. Bakunin would be instrumental in not only formally establishing an anarchist movement, but also identifying that movement as a supporter of revolutionary change, and, in some respects, terrorist tactics. Born close to

Moscow, Bakunin's rebellious nature brought him to Paris by 1840, where he met both Proudhon and Marx. Both he and Marx became admirers of the ideas being developed by the French anarchist, and while Marx would later break sharply with Proudhon, Bakunin did only to a degree. The latter, in fact, was never a strongly original thinker and his differences with Proudhon were mainly a reflection of numbers, the growing size of the working class in Europe, and of tactics.

Bakunin was always an activist. His reputation began to grow after the revolutions of 1848, then during numerous subsequent attempts at revolt by very diverse groups. His revolutionary fervor led to his arrest and imprisonment in Germany, Austria, Russia, and ultimately exile in Siberia. After years of harsh, debilitating incarceration Bakunin made a dramatic escape from Russia and returned to the struggles in the west. This added to his legendary stature as he embarked on new efforts to overthrow the capitalist system. Of particular importance would be his efforts to involve the Slavic peoples of Russia and the Latin population of southern Europe in the struggle. It was in these regions where anarchism would gain its greatest support.

One of the two areas where Bakunin differed from Proudhon was in promoting the idea of much larger collectives of workers forming self-sufficient production and consumption units. As with Proudhon's mutualist groups, distribution of goods and services would be based on the labor contributed. The second area of difference was in promoting revolutionary activism to achieve anarchism. He founded international organizations, first in Italy, and later in Switzerland. From Switzerland, Bakunin directed the organizations that would contest with Marxist groups that led to the split of the First International Workingmen's Association and the subsequent rise of international anarchism. Bakunin's differences with Marx stemmed from the anarchists' rejection of the communist idea of a workers' political movement and a transitional state, the dictatorship of the proletariat, before the achievement of a stateless society. Besides this animosity to the

Marxist concept of a centralized, heirarchical system, there were deep personal differences between the two men.

Bakunin also left his mark on international anarchism by identifying it with terrorism. For a time he fell under the sway of Sergei Nechayev, a young Russian exile, who was a fanatic revolutionary—not an anarchist but an advocate of revolutionary dictatorship. Bakunin allowed his name to be used on a number of pamphlets (and indeed wrote some of them), that argued passionately for the use of indiscriminant extermination in the name of the revolution. Though the direct involvement of Bakunin in the development of these ideas is debated, there would subsequently be a violent element identified with the anarchist movement. The idea of "propaganda by the deed" not only appealed to some individuals in the movement, but it led to attempts by others to rationalize acts of violence, as well as to the execution of numerous spectacular violent acts themselves. Furthermore, it would contribute to the popular stereotype of anarchism worldwide, and when would-be revolutionaries in Mexico and the United States were labeled, or professed themselves to be, anarchists, the image projected was often one of the bomb-throwing, knife-wielding terrorist.

No one could be further removed from this stereotype than the kind and gentle Russian aristocrat, Pyotr Kropotkin, who succeeded Bakunin as the leading advocate of anarchism, and who probably had the greatest influence on Práxedis Guerrero and the Mexican anarchists led by Ricardo Flores Magón. Born to landed wealth in Russia, Kropotkin became a follower of Bakunin. His support of anarchist causes led to prison terms in both France and Russia, culminated by, like Bakunin, a dramatic escape from Russia. By the 1880s Kropotkin was settled in England, where he stayed until returning to his native land after the Russian Revolution. A trained geographer and a skilled naturalist, Kropotkin gave anarchism a scientific underpinning for its wildly optimistic view of human nature. His reading of Charles Darwin, in contrast to the "Social Darwinists" and their justification of unbridled selfishness, led him to argue that Darwin's work demonstrated that spontaneous cooperation was more important for survival. He expressed these ideas most completely in his book *Mutual Aid*.

Cooperation would be developed through a return to the community, the commune for Kropotkin being a voluntary association that unites groups of like interests. These groups network with other groups in a cooperative manner, replacing the state. Kropotkin's ideas came to be known as anarchist communism and differ from Proudhon's mutualism and Bakunin's collectivism in one very significant respect. Both of the latter argued for systems of distribution within the community based on the individual worker's contribution. To Kropotkin, this represented a compulsion, a creation of property—some workers would have more than others because they produced more—that had no place in a voluntary society. Kropotkin proposed instead that distribution be based on need: "from each according to his means, to each according his needs." The ideas of anarchist communism, sometimes styled anarcho-communism, were developed in detail in Kropotkin's *The Conquest of Bread*.

To achieve his ideal, Kropotkin believed the state had to be destroyed. Before coming to England, he had supported revolutionary causes and he continued to believe that revolution was inevitable, but through most of his life Kropotkin was far removed from the image of the anarchist terrorist. He believed "that it was by means of the printed word that the cause of the revolution could best be served and that a clandestine pamphlet was worth more than the terrorist's bomb or the assassin's dagger."[3] Flores Magón most certainly must have shared that belief—in contrast Guerrero felt the need to back up his words with deeds. Kropotkin never tried to organize anarchist groups or movements, although many of his followers did. The Italian Errico Malatesta was one who did, and his writings had considerable influence on the Mexican anarchists. Spanish anarchism, also important in Mexico, was less influenced by Kropotkin—

more by Proudhon and Bakunin. It was a Spaniard, Tarrida de Mármol, who was one of the first to try to reconcile the various anarchist traditions in calling for an anarchy without adjectives. Malatesta took up some of these same arguments.[4]

The historian John Mason Hart traced the development of anarchism in Mexico, seeing parallels to the European experience in the rise of industrial society and the corresponding growth of an urban work force in the second half of the nineteenth century. A Greek immigrant, Plotino Rhodakanaty, was the first organizer of an anarchist working class movement in Mexico. In the late-nineteenth century anarchism in Mexico received a tremendous boost from the large number of Spanish immigrants, many leaving Spain because of their anarchist activities in that country. Hart argues that anarchism was much more important for industrial workers in Mexico than Marxism until after the success of the Russian Revolution.[5] More recently, however, Hart revised some of his views on the origins of anarchism in Mexico, stressing that a tradition of mutualism and cooperativism among Mexican workers created support for an essentially anarchist society even before the introduction of European anarchist ideas.

Tracing communal working and living arrangements through several of the precolombian civilizations, Hart suggests that the Spanish conquest reenforced some of the Indian practices in rural areas where the viceregal state, the church, and the indigenous population sponsored the development of community landholdings and mutualist assistance societies known as *cajas de communidad*. As cities were built or rebuilt after the conquest, many of these traditions were carried forward in artisan guilds, again featuring Spanish practices merging with indigenous customs. Consequently, long before the development of industrial capitalism, "the Mexican working class had a long and pervasive experience with local self-help organizations, guilds, the practice of mutual aid . . ." all of which would indicate a receptive climate for the introduction of anarchism.[6]

While Hart documents the development of working class reactions to the nineteenth-century origins of industrialization in Mexico in a manner that convincingly demonstrates many of the generic roots of Mexican anarchism, the *magonista* embracement of the philosophy requires more thought. For one thing, none of the principal leaders had any significant contact with working class groups until after they left Mexico. It seems most likely that their attraction to anarchism came from direct reading of the works of the European anarchists and their disciples. Ricardo Flores Magón, a Oaxaca *mestizo*, came out of the communal indigenous traditions of a small village in his native state, which would no doubt have its influence throughout his life.[7] Still, he probably had his introduction to anarchism as a student in Mexico City in the 1890s. When he united with the liberal movement emerging out of San Luis Potosí about the turn of the century, he came in contact with people such as Camilo Arriaga, Antonio Díaz Soto y Gama, Juan Sarabia, and others who were reading, thinking about, and discussing all manner of radical political theory. Librado Rivera wrote that Ricardo was familiar with the works of Bakunin and Kropotkin by 1900, but that would not necessarily make him an anarchist; he was also familiar with the works of Karl Marx. He must have debated these issues with the other Liberals, because immediately after they first entered the United States in 1904, differences between Flores Magón and Arriaga over politics began to split the movement.[8]

In St. Louis the leaders of the *Partido Liberal Mexicano* came into contact with anarchists such as Emma Goldman and the Spaniard Francisco Bazora, who became close to Ricardo at the time. On the other hand, the *Programa y Manifesto* of the PLM in 1906 was not an anarchist document. Instead, this program, calling for a revolution and outlining a new government, was grounded in Mexican liberalism modified by nationalistic concerns which had risen out of the favoritism to foreigners during the Porfiriato. It was not until after the failures of the 1906 revolt, and with Flores Magón incarcerated from 1907 to 1910, that he began to espouse anarchism openly. His treatment at the hands of government, as well as the time to think that being imprisoned gave him, probably contributed to the evolutionary development of his commitment to anarchism. No public pronouncement of belief in anarchy was made by Flores Magón until 1911.9

This does not mean there is no evidence of a sympathy toward anarchism much earlier. However, when agents or representatives of the Mexican and United States governments or private detectives employed by Mexico referred to the *magonistas* as anarchists, as they did often from 1906 on, likely as not the term was being used in a pejorative sense or simply as another word for revolutionary. Many of the *magonistas* so labeled, men such as Antonio I. Villarreal and Manuel Sarabia, were definitely not anarchists, and, especially in Villarreal's case, would split with Flores Magón over the issue. Práxedis Guerrero, who joined the movement later, seems to have come to a belief in the ideas of anarchism from his own readings and his own experiences, and his anarchism influenced everything he did.

Guerrero received a good education in the schools of León, studying the classics, learning Latin, and generally benefiting from the traditional curriculum of better private schools in Porfirian Mexico. The social and cultural life of Mexico in this era was very consciously modeled on the European, especially the French, experience. Consequently, Guerrero, with his interest in philosophy and history, would be drawn to reading the works of the French *philosophes* and studies of the French Revolution—the very sources that gave rise to anarchism in Europe. Guerrero was also fascinated by his study of the works and theories of Charles Darwin, which Kropotkin used to demonstrate the importance of cooperation in evolution. What this educational background suggests is that by the time Guerrero was introduced to the ideas of Proudhon, Bakunin, Kropotkin, and other anarchist theorists, he was already well grounded in many of the intellectual sources of their ideas.

While he was still serving in Bernardo Reyes' Second Military Reserve, Guerrero presumably became familiar with some of the opposition newspapers. At the same time he had read many of the leading Russia writers. Among such writers were not only the leading anarchist theorists like Bakunin and Kropotkin, but also Leo Tolstoy. Tolstoy was in every major belief an anarchist, particularly in the last three decades of his life. However, he refused to call himself one because he repudiated violence. He simplified anarchism as a philosophy advocating violence. Even Kropotkin, whom he admired a great deal, argued that revolution was inevitable. Tolstoy called himself a true Christian in his non-violent approach. Guerrero, styling himself a military man, supported the necessity of revolution to overthrow the Mexican government and to bring on anarchism. Yet many of his personal habits seemed to be patterned after the ideas of Tolstoy, including his vegetarianism.

In the summer of 1904, when Práxedis spent time in Puebla with his convalescing father, he read extensively from the works of Jean-Jacques Rousseau. He also visited from time to time in many of the small villages around Puebla, where, despite the harshness of life for many, Guerrero might have witnessed aspects of a happy primitive world and considerable mutual cooperation—virtues extolled by Rousseau. During this time or shortly after the return to Guanajuato, Guerrero decided to leave Mexico to experience life in the United States. Although he had worked in San Luis Potosí for some months in 1900, and possibly had been in contact with workers advocating radical ideas, he was still a member of the landed elite. He became one of the working class by choice after leaving Mexico—an action that accelerated his radical thinking.

In the United States, Guerrero worked for the most part in areas where there were large numbers of Mexican laborers. Copies of his first paper, *Alba Roja*, "Red Dawn," published for workers on the docks of San Francisco, are unavailable, but the title reeks of a radical orientation. In Morenci, Arizona, he took the lead in organizing workers and in 1906 affiliated with the *Partido Liberal Mexicano* in St. Louis. His initiation into the *PLM* was through Manuel Sarabia, a socialist, not an anarchist, and the *PLM* agenda gave no evidence of anarchist leanings at that time. During this time Guerrero was said to be inclined toward "study and politics."[10] The "study" included his consistent and general interest in philosophy and history, but now also anarchist writers such as Malatesta, the Spaniards Francisco Ferrer y Guardia and Fernando Tarrida de Mármol, as well as Bakunin and Kropotkin. Some saw Guerrero as an apostle of Kropotkin, often carrying copies of his works wherever he went.[11]

In 1907 Guerrero began to write for *Revolución*, then published in Los Angeles. It is noteworthy that while his earliest writings in *Revolución* could not be said to be specifically anarchistic, the newspaper also carried articles about Kropotkin and Spanish translations of some of Kropotkin's writings. In the fall of 1907, when Práxedis moved to California to be more directly involved in the production of the paper, he had his first face-to-face meeting with Ricardo Flores Magón. There is no indication that they met often or that they had any extensive discussions of ideology. Flores Magón was in jail with Antonio Villarreal, never an anarchist, and with Librado Rivera, who would closely follow Flores Magón in every ideological twist and turn. At this point, it could even be argued that it was questionable who would instruct whom in anarchism, as Guerrero seems to have read as extensively as Flores Magón. By 1908, both discussed anarchism openly and the elder *PLM* leader took on some aspects of a "teacher."

At the end of May 1908, with Ricardo still in the Los Angeles County jail, Práxedis went to El Paso to assume direction of the anticipated revolution. In early June, Enrique Flores Magón, from hiding in Los Angeles, wrote Guerrero pleading with him not to risk capture by crossing into Mexico. Writing "although we are anarchists," the younger Flores Magón still thought "we should consider ourselves as leaders of the liberal army."[12] Shortly thereafter, Ricardo wrote a lengthy letter to both

Guerrero and his brother Enrique. Composed with difficulty over the course of several days—writing was difficult because of the manner in which Flores Magón was confined and because of the futile efforts to keep his writing a secret from his jailers—Ricardo outlined the anarchist nature of the upcoming revolt. Although addressed to both Práxedis and Enrique, the latter part of the letter seemed to be directed primarily to his brother.

Ricardo wrote that if the revolution succeeded under the ideals of the Liberal movement, it would not achieve their goals. After the revolution would come the congresses, representing all interests and opinions, to legislate change. Even if by a miracle—for the lawmakers were rarely those who made the revolution—changes were enacted into law, they would still not guarantee success for the revolution. The landowners, the owners of companies and factories, would all resist, forcing compromises in the revolutionary program. The people, without bread, would be forced to accept these compromises. "As anarchists we know all this very well," Flores Magón wrote, they could expect only so much from any government. They must work to see that this revolution gave as many benefits as possible to the people.

> In order to obtain great benefits for the people, effective benefits, to work as anarchists would easily crush us, yet for the same purpose we subject ourselves to leaders. All is reduced to a mere question of tactics. If from the first we had called ourselves anarchists, no one, or not but a few, would have listened to us. Without calling ourselves anarchists we have gone on planting in minds hatred against the possessing class and against the governmental caste. No liberal party in the world has the anti-capitalist tendencies of that about to produce a revolution in Mexico, and this has been achieved without saying that we are anarchists, even though we would not have succeeded had we entitled ourselves, not anarchists as we are, but simply socialists. All, then, is a question of tactics.

We must give land to the people in the course of the revolution; so that the poor will not be deceived. There is not a single government which can benefit the country against the interests of the bourgeoisie. This you know well as anarchists, and for that reason I do not need to demonstrate it with reasoning or examples. We must also give the people possession of the factories, mines, etc. In order not to turn the entire nation against us, we must follow the same tactics that we have practiced with such success: we will continue calling ourselves liberals in the course of the revolution but in reality we will be propagating anarchy and executing anarchistic acts. We must strip away the property of the bourgeoisie and restore it to the people.

It was perhaps an example of the eternal optimism of the anarchists for Flores Magón to write of anything they had "practiced with such success," but he went to describe how the revolution would unfold. On land distribution, he wrote:

it would be unfair to give all lands to the workers of the land because then many would be left with nothing. Workers of landed property will be given the land they actually work, reserving the remainder for the poor . . . those that want lands that are not now being used, upon seeing the excellence of community work practiced by the redeemed laborers (instead of working the land individually), will want to work in common also, and in that way there will be no need of fragmenting the land in parcels. This will spare the Junta the hateful work of giving to each who requests it a piece of land.

It would further the cause of anarchy, he thought, that the necessity of avoiding widespread hunger would bring the production of goods in common.

Through the mutual production and exchange of goods there

would be surpluses to support the military. The workers themselves should be armed to protect "what the revolution has given them from the assaults of the soldiers of tyranny, and the probable attack of the gringos or some other nations." Bourgeoisie foreigners in the country would not be bothered until almost all the people "have something material to defend," and then "we will see that there will not be one that does not hold a rifle." Flores Magón expected many Spanish and Italian anarchists to come to join the revolution when they saw how it was developing. "We must cultivate international relationships, but not with the government but with labor organizations all over the world, be it simply trade unionists, socialists, or anarchists." Relations with governments, he wrote, would bring "a sea of commitments that take away from the revolution its very special character."

Writing the letter over several days, often in physical discomfort, Flores Magón repeated himself on several issues. He felt it was important that anarchist literature—pamphlets, books, and papers—be distributed widely and that anarchist agitators be infiltrated among the workers. Unrealistically he suggested:

> Only the anarchists will know we are anarchists, and we will advise them that they don't call us anarchists so as not to frighten so many imbeciles that hold ideals like ours in the depths of their minds, but without knowing they are anarchist ideals, so accustomed are they to hearing of the anarchists in such unfavorable terms. Rather than imbeciles, they are ignorant. We should not be unjust.
>
> I dream of great, effective conquests during the revolution. We must not hesitate. It is very possible that our revolution will break the European equilibrium and those proletarians will decide to do what we do. Perhaps if we carried out what I propose the European powers will turn on us, but that will be the last act of the governmental farce, because I am sure that our brothers on the other side of the ocean will not let us perish.[13]

Like most anarchists Flores Magón was better on the attack than he was in formulating exactly what would follow the elimination of government. This letter, however, did reveal he had thought extensively about how the revolution might develop.

Guerrero, unfettered by prison bars, actively plotted the revolt, while continuing to develop his own anarchist thoughts to justify the need for revolution. When Guerrero first began to write for *Revolución,* most of his essays were directed at generating support for a revolution planned for the next year, 1908; other pieces were general attacks on the Díaz system. In 1908, he became the leader in the field trying to bring on the revolution, a position about which he seemed to have mixed emotions. His descriptions of the uprising in Viesca and the attack on Las Vacas reveal a great interest in the military aspects of the revolt, and he personally led the attack on Palomas, which he also described dramatically. His letters through 1909 and 1910 addressed to various supporters in Texas and other areas reveal a confidence and sense of ease in command. On the other hand, in 1909, he told Jesús María Rangel, that he thought "a popular revolution should be spontaneous, without leaders." Further, he said he was not simply an enemy of Díaz, but "I am an anarchist; I don't fight because I hate government, but for love of a free humanity."[14]

As his anarchist ideals became stronger, Guerrero was more and more concerned with eliminating the system that produced oppression rather than the oppressors themselves. As the twenty-seven-year-old revolutionary told his sister in a letter in April 1910:

> No one should get angry against those who caused my personal wrongs. I do not hold them in esteem, but I am far from hating them. I know that they are the product of the fatal social conditions in which we live, that they in turn are also victims, and their hatred against me, logical and excus-

able from the point of view of instinctive passions, is perfectly absurd judged by the philosphical reason that is vastly superior to that vileness and superficiality. . . . When I was younger and had a brain more ardent than reflective, I did not feel this way, but today through the mercy of the winds that have whipped me, the heaven of my mind has been robbed of clouds, and I feel differently.

Guerrero saw all wrongs—"cruelties and injustices"—as the result of determinism, and consequently hatred toward the perpetrator of evils annulled human intelligence.

This does not mean I am a Christian and present my cheeks to the fists of anyone who wants to slap me—none of that: I defend myself against my enemies, but without hatred, without the madness of hatred, just as I defend myself against an illness that attacks me, as I would fight against the waters that threatened to swallow me. Behind my immediate enemies whose hands harass me, I see the causes that throw them against me. I go toward those causes because the improvement of the current disastrous condition of Society, will eliminate those causes.[15]

Many of the ideas in this letter were developed at length in some of his published writings.

Most of his essays appeared in the revived *Regeneración* in September, October, and November of 1910, just before he went to his death at Janos. In discussing "The Purpose of the Revolution," Guerrero explained that killing the tyrant would not eliminate the tyranny, because tyrannies are products of social ills. "Tyranny is the logical result of a social disease, whose present remedy is the revolution, since the pacific resistance of the doctrine of Tolstoy, would only produce in these times, the annihilation of the few who might ever have understood or practiced its simplicity." To those who might confuse revolution with war, Guerrero wrote that wars were characterized by "hatred and national or personal ambitions," while revolutions were "abrupt upheavals" toward improvement. "Wars can be fought against a man, but never a revolution," which creates an environment "for the development and the expansion of all beings."[16]

In "The True Interest of the Bourgeoisie and the Proletariat," Guerrero asserted that "the transformation of the present system is unavoidable and that it would best serve their interest [the bourgeoisie] to facilitate that transformation." Arguing that personal improvement and satisfaction were the goals of every human, Guerrero wrote that the bourgeoisie were chained to false interests:

> Stealing the bread from others means placing one's own sustenance in certain danger. Snatching away the happiness of others means chaining oneself. Destroying other people's happiness in order to fabricate our own from its remains is nonsense. Because to attempt to raise one's own happiness over the misery and grief of others is comparable to wanting to fortify a building by destroying its foundation. Nevertheless, most of the people deceived by the appearance of their false interests, walk through the world like that, in search of their welfare, under the banner of this absurd principle: to harm, in order to benefit.[17]

He developed his ideas on tyrannies as products of the "natural law of determinism" in his "The Means and the End." Of tyrants and common criminals, he wrote that tyranny is most forgivable, because a

> common wrongdoer can commit his misdeeds without the complicity of his victims; a despot cannot live or tyrannize without the cooperation of his [victims]—or a numerous part of them. Tyranny is the crime of the unconscious collectivists against themselves and must be attacked as a social

disease by means of the revolution, considering the death of the tyrants as an unavoidable incident of the struggle, an incident, and nothing more, not an act of justice. . . . The end to all revolutions, as we have said many times, is to guarantee for everyone the right to life, by destroying the causes of misery, of ignorance and despotism; by disdaining the uproar of sentimentality of the theoretical humanists.[18]

In a piece entitled "Working," Práxedis, after characterizing the labor of many types of individuals—good and bad, rich and poor—described his own role as he saw it:

> And so, gloomy and pensive, the revolutionary meditates; he leans over any old piece of paper and he writes strong phrases that hurt, that shake, that vibrate like the bugles of a storm; he wanders and he ignites with the flames of his words the extinguished consciences; he sows rebellion and discontent; he forges the weapons of freedom with the iron from the chains that he destroys; restlessly, he goes through the crowds taking to them the ideas and the hopes; he works, he works. What does he work for? So that the peasant can enjoy the products of his care, and the miner, without sacrificng his life, can have plenty of bread; so that the humble seamstress can sew dresses for herself and can also enjoy the sweet things in life; so that love can be the feeling that, honoring and perpetuating the species, can join two free beings; so that neither the king of industry, nor the judge, nor the henchmen spend their lives working in detriment of mankind; so that the priest and the prostitute both disappear, so that tyranny, despotism and ignorance all die; so that justice and freedom, rationally making all human beings equal, can make them into the solidaristic builders of a common welfare; so that everyone has, without having to descend into degradation, an assured right to life.[19]

All of these essays were published in *Regeneración* while the *magonistas* were still calling themselves liberals and trying to establish a position in what was obviously going to be the long-sought overthrow of the Mexican government. The analyses and arguments used by Guerrero were clearly anarchistic, and recognized as such by anyone with any knowledge of anarchism. What he wrote, romanticized by what he did in dying young at the outset of the Mexican Revolution, helped make Práxedis an internationally recognized figure in anarchism. Moreover, his socialist friend, Manuel Sarabia, circulated Guerrero's writings in Europe, where perhaps he came to be known better than he was in either the United States or Mexico. His restless nature could not keep him out of the fighting but, as with both Kropotkin and Flores Magón, he characterized the work of the revolutionary as writing.

"WRITING, WRITING, WRITING"

As a leader on the battlefield, Práxedis Guerrero does not loom large in the history of the Mexican Revolution. The attempt at revolt in 1908 fizzled out because of inadequate arms, too few *revoltosos*, and the hostile opposition and infiltration of two governments. The two assaults Guerrero led personally were acts of desperation or frustration—the first costing the life of his dear friend Francisco Manrique and the second his own life. Yet, the supposed remains of "General Práxedis G. Guerrero" were brought to Chihuahua city for burial with honors by the state of Chihuahua in 1935.[1] It was not Guerrero the "General" being honored but Guerrero the precursor of revolution, Guerrero the selfless defender of the downtrodden, and, above all, Guerrero the writer.

The writings of Guerrero were published in three primary sources: the newspaper *Revolución*, published in Los Angeles in 1907 and 1908; *Punto Rojo*, the paper Guerrero published in El Paso for about nine months in 1909 and 1910; and finally the famed Flores Magón newspaper, *Regeneración*, which began its third life in Los Angeles in 1910. Few copies of *Revolución* and *Punto Rojo* have survived so most of his known writings come from *Regeneración* and were published between 1910 and early 1911. Some essays were published posthumously, though many had been published earlier in *Punto Rojo, Revolución*, or one of the many small Spanish language periodicals published intermittently in the southwestern United States in the years before the Mexican Revolution. It is not possible to determine the exact dates he wrote even the published works. Not being able to examine the works in any definite chronological order presents problems in attempting to reach conclusions or make interpretations about Guerrero's intellectual development.[2]

In the 1920s, as part of an effort to secure the release of Ricardo Flores Magón, who was imprisoned in the United States federal penitentiary in Leavenworth, Kansas, a group in Mexico City began to republish works of the *magonistas*. The *Grupo Cultural "Ricardo Flores Magón"* was directed by Nicolás T. Bernal, with support from Librado Rivera. Although it was not publicized, the publication of inexpensive paperback editions was made possible by the Mexican Ministry of Education headed by José Vasconcelos. Included among the editions was a 1924 collection entitled *Práxedis G. Guerrero*, with the subtitle *Artículos literarios y de combate; pensamientos; crónicas revolucionarias, etc.* Flores Magón died in November 1922, but the project was underway before that time and received his warm support.[3]

Some of these same works received wider circulation when

they were included in a collection edited by Armando Bartra and called *Regeneración, 1900-1918*, published first in 1977 and reprinted several times, including a 1986 edition by the modern *Secretaría de Educación Pública*.4 In 1977 the most complete edition of Guerrero's writings to date was published through the efforts of a León, Guanajuato, libertarian, Omar Cortés. Titled *Práxedis G. Guerrero: Artículos de Combate*, the new volume included most of the contents of the 1924 publication and included articles gleaned from copies of *Revolución* and *Punto Rojo* discovered in Mexican archives. This same collection was also brought out in 1977 by the state of Guanajuato under the title *Vocación de Libertad* with a prologue by José Muñoz Cota. Omar Cortés and Chantal López, through their *Ediciones Antorcha* in Mexico City, have republished most of the old *Grupo Cultural "Ricardo Flores Magón"* works and added numerous publications on both the *magonistas* and anarchism.5

Guerrero as a writer poses some interesting problems for anyone attempting to analyze his work. Although the *Partido Liberal Mexicano* drew most of its support in the United States from poorly paid and little educated Mexican workers, Guerrero's prose was often flowery, complex, and not easily understood. Some of his composition tends to be "poetic." For example James Cockcroft, in his excellent study of the intellectual antecedents of the Mexican Revolution, wrote that "poet and Anarchist" Guerrero "forsook all his family and wealth for a life of poverty, poetry, revolutionary combat, and martyrdom."6 Ralph Chaplin, the American radical whose activities on behalf on the Industrial Workers of the World landed him in Leavenworth, became a friend of Flores Magón in his last days. In his autobiography Chaplin who had spent time in Mexico, wrote of receiving *Regeneración* when it was published in Los Angeles: "I translated poems by the Mexican poet, Praxedes [sic] Guerrero, into English whenever they appeared." Later, in Leavenworth, he wrote that he and Ricardo in their spare time "were working together on translations of Praxedes [sic]

Guerrero's revolutionary poems. He had a huge admiration for this young Mexican poet. . . ."[7] Flores Magón referred to Guerrero as an "exceptional man, poet, philosopher, and revolutionary."[8] Other scholars have picked up these references to the poetry of Guerrero, but the fact remains: Práxedis never wrote any poetry as the term is generally understood. Each reader decides whether his works were poetic.

Writing, particularly for periodicals, appealed to Guerrero from a very early age. While still a teenager he published occasionally in the newspapers of León and San Felipe, the major population centers closest to the family hacienda. He became a correspondent in León for the Mexico City paper, *Diario del Hogar*. He was in the United States less than six months before he began publishing *Alba Roja* in San Francisco. His first major contact with the *Partido Liberal Mexicano* was through Manuel Sarabia, a journalist. Soon both Guerrero and Sarabia would be directing the *PLM* periodical, *Revolución*, and then, with Flores Magón and others in jail or prison, Guerrero became the principal writer for the movement.

In his first essays, with the *PLM* still reeling from the failures and subsequent arrests in 1906, Guerrero lashed out at Porfirio Díaz and predicted a successful revolution. In "Justice!," first distributed in loose sheets on the streets of Douglas, Arizona, and then published in *Revolución*, he recounted the kidnapping of Manuel Sarabia. Charging Díaz with manipulating the episode, Guerrero called on Mexicans to "clean the Porfirian stain" from their country. "Let's erase the word tyranny from the fatherland and replace it with another on which rests the only peace acceptable for man: JUSTICE!"[9] Despite Guerrero's concern with the Sarabia case, many of his early pieces did not deal with specific events. In September 1907, about the time he and Sarabia moved to Los Angeles to take over the paper, his article "Make Way" appeared in *Revolución*:

> Out of the cluster of clouds that the hurricane whirls

around to darken the skies, comes the flaming sword wielded by an invisible arm, and with dazzling zig-zags writes on the page roaring with black smoke, the words MAKE WAY! And as the shadow becomes darker, the sword glows even brighter.

Out of the squall of hatred that besieges us; out of the black bosom of the tempests that the tyranny unleashes over our foreheads, comes the invulnerable sword of the Idea and writes with the lightning of the word, in the very heart of darkness, pages of honor to the inextinguishable cry: MAKE WAY!

After a few more paragraphs in the same vein, Guerrero reached for some Mexican history:

The old saber of Ayutla and the Reform jumps impatiently in its rusty sheath . . . MAKE WAY! to the heroic weapons of the redeeming struggles.

We arrive with serene hearts to the doors of glorious death and we knock with the hilt of the steel, crying: MAKE WAY![10]

While many of essays tended to be allegorical, at other times he urged his readers to action, as in "Let's Work, Fighters!":
"Walk faster, multiply the action. While our fatherland is enslaved we should not take even an hour to rest. While the jails deprive our fallen brothers of movement and light, it is a crime to stand in the shackles of indolence." This article, published not long after the arrest of Ricardo Flores Magón, Antonio I. Villarreal, and Librado Rivera, continued with a sense of urgency throughout. "We cannot stop for moment . . . we cannot sleep . . . fight without a truce . . . don't permit an increase in the list of sacrificed without reducing the number of sacrificers. . . . If we cannot reach liberty walking, we must jump. . . ." In conclusion, Práxedis wrote: "Double the labor, we will rest

later when the body of the old buffoon of Tuxtepec, on the end of a rope, serves as the lead weight for the architect of the future to raise the walls of the houses of the people."[11]

In the same issue of *Revolución* "Listen," began quietly and built to a dramatic finish:

> Do you hear it? It is the wind rustling the branches in the mysterious forest. The gust of wind of the future, which wakens the quiet and sleepy underbrush; it is the first sigh of the virgin grove receiving on its bowed head the kiss of the impetuous Aeolus. . . .
>
> It is the breath of the Revolution.
>
> Do you feel it? It is the quaking of granite cracking to pieces, beaten by the iron fists of Pluto; it is the heart of the world beating beneath its enormous chest; it is the fiery spirit of a giant who breaks from his prison to hurl curses of flame into space.
>
> It is the trembling announcing the birth of a crater of a volcano.
>
> Do you feel it? It is the vibrations made by the hammers of the gods. . . .
>
> It is the force of the Revolution advancing.[12]

In December 1907, Guerrero wrote of the blows the movement had absorbed with so many leaders now in jail or in hiding but made clear that he would continue to fight on, pen in hand. From "The Boxer": "Our silence can be obtained only with death, but even so, the rebel pen we grasp will implacably continue cutting the mantle of Caesar to show the sword the way to his rotten heart; the immortal spirit of the revolution, identified with the sword, will find a hundred hands prepared to replace us in the fight." In conclusion Guerrero defiantly wrote: "We are standing; we will kneel before no power. We face the enemy; we will not turn our backs before any danger."[13]

Guerrero compared Díaz and his accomplices to the lowest

forms of life crawling out of the slime in "Vile Hatreds." They could not walk higher than the reptiles. They never fall on their enemies from on high like an eagle, but, instead they wait in the thicket for a naked foot to bite. Continuing the natural history theme, he wrote: "We are not in the lair of the tiger, but in the nest of the rattlesnake. To fight against tigers would be beautiful. To crush snakes is repugnant."[14]

Shortly after this article appeared early in 1908, *Revolución* was suppressed, but was briefly revived in late April of that year. For the most part Guerrero was without an outlet for his passionate concerns until he launched *Punto Rojo* in El Paso in August 1909. On the masthead Guerrero wrote: "I am not merchandise, I am an idea; and ideas are defended, not bought." It is remarkable that Guerrero was able to keep *Punto Rojo* going for nine months since he was a wanted man, under indictment for neutrality law violations and had to work to support himself. The newspaper began as a very small-format weekly, not always published every week, but in time it grew to a standard sized newspaper. It was very important to Práxedis to have this means of expressing his ideas, although the circumstances often led to some hurried efforts that were not his best work.[15]

In one of the first offerings he discussed "Passivity and Rebellion," with the obvious conclusion of "Passivity never! Rebellion, now and forever." The argument was actually more complex than the conclusion indicates; Guerrero was denouncing elections and other evolutionary methods of change. It was probably one of his earliest statements in support of anarchism, though naturally not labeled so.[16] The same issue of *Punto Rojo* carried other articles on the theme. Guerrero wrote often about passivity, undoubtedly a reflection of his frustrations in attempting to spur uprisings on either side of the border. In "Beggar," he compared begging for bread to begging for liberty. "Beggar of liberty . . . Beggar of bread . . . do not beg anymore, demand it. Stop waiting: take it!"[17] Práxedis tried to stimulate actions through appeals to women in "Whom Do You Love, Women?"

in that same issue, writing: "Whom do you love? Whom do you love? To whom do you give that tenderness that only an honorable and free man knows how to value, to deserve and conserve, to increase and defend?"[18]

It is clear that Guerrero's audience for *Punto Rojo* was the Mexican population in the United States. In the issue of August 29, 1909, where attacks on passivity appeared, he addressed the possibility that Porfirio Díaz would be invited to El Paso to meet with United States President William Howard Taft. Entitling it simply "Residents of El Paso," he asked "Do you want to rejoice in the disgusting presence of the assassin-tyrant Porfirio Díaz? Do you think the visit of this shady bandit honors us?" After recounting some of what he called the crimes of Díaz, including actions against the *magonistas* such as the kidnapping of Manuel Sarabia, Guerrero wrote that the Mexican leader probably would be afraid to come to the border even if asked. Still, he told his readers they must protest:

> In Mexico there is an excuse for those who pretend to coexist with the Tyrant; that excuse is terror. But you do not have this excuse, you cannot have it, and if you accept any part given you in this degrading farce, there will be no valid subterfuge; not even the water of one hundred biblical floods will remove the stain you will have thrown on yourselves.
>
> Defend dignity or wait for me to burn your face with the word that will distinguish you in the future: Wretches![19]

Guerrero wasted no chance to exhort, shame or inspire the Mexicans on the frontier to action against the Porfiriato. In the issue dated September 16, 1909, the ninety-ninth anniversary of the Father Miguel Hidalgo's call for revolt that is celebrated as Mexican Independence Day, he drew parallels to the current situation. In an article titled "Anniversary," he noted how the "humble, the exploited of 1810" had rallied around the standard of revolt and soon it would be the "Centenary of that illegal act." And now "1810 accuses; 1810 interrogates. What do you respond, Mexicans?" To Práxedis, the "work of the ragmuffins of that time, instead of progressing, had drowned in the apathy and the fear of their descendents."

> Mexico has gone back further by train than from where it left barefoot.
> The celebration sounds profoundly ironic.
> We live under the claw of the fox of the North, we barely breathe for fear of provoking the anger of a senile despot; autonomy and liberty are two miserable paradoxes for the Mexican people, all the same they think of commemorative fiestas for deeds that were worthy and glorious.
> The slaves directed by their boatswains sing songs of victory to the liberty they had renounced and to the bravery they had exchanged for meekness.
> Wordiness, smoke, genuflections, such is the ritual of the historic moment which confronts us prescribed for the enthusiasms of those who hunger for illusions, also for the grave-diggers of the Mexican race.
> Will the sun of the Centenary burn the backs of a flock of sheep or will it kiss the proud forehead of a people?
> Answer, Mexicans; there is still time to wash our tatters to shine at the first light of the Centenary of the liberating effort of 1810.[20]

Shortly after he began *Punto Rojo*, Guerrero had to flee El Paso to avoid arrest, having been charged with violation of United States neutrality laws as the result of the attempted revolts of 1908. The paper continued, not always regularly or punctually, but he contributed to it whenever and however he could. At the same time Guerrero wrote letters of instruction to *PLM* faithful, issuing manifestos, personally rallying individuals and groups to the cause, and trying to work enough to maintain himself and his newspaper. His writing suffered and there was a scarcity of productivity from Práxedis' pen until September 1910 when he went to Los Angeles and began to write for *Regeneración*, revived by the newly freed Ricardo Flores Magón and his associates.

Punto Rojo was suppressed by authorities in El Paso in May 1910; shortly before, Práxedis had written to a sister about his composition:

> Unfortunately, in this fight one must use terms of argument similar to those that oppose us; philosophy does not penetrate a rock, you have use a crowbar and and a hammer. When writing pages destined to energize the people, I often become violent and use a language that intimately I reject; but the sublimely cold language of philosophical truth is not the most fit language to awaken the enthusiasm that every revolution needs in order to achieve victory.[21]

In *Regeneración*, Guerrero continued to try to stir Mexicans in the United States to action. In the first issue, in "Something Else," he argued that the exploitation of and discrimination against Mexicans in the United States was directly related to conditions in Mexico. Mexicans accepted the insults from a racist society because the economic opportunities fed their families, something they could not do in Mexico. Even that was changing, as Guerrero recounted actions in Texas, Oklahoma, Arizona and other southwestern states taken against the "passive and indifferent workers." "Peonage, horrible peonage," he wrote, "left behind in the fogs of ignominious memory floating in the huts of the haciendas was sliding in this direction." The migrants left misery and hunger in Mexico and now "shame, humiliation and hunger . . . the universal companions of the impotent" faced them in the United States. The "something else," implied in the article, was a call for revolution as the way to escape these "two hungers."[22]

The next week Práxedis explained "The True Interest of the Bourgeoisie and the Proletariat." He contended that many people spent their time defending false interests, for example: "The privileged are opposed, with all the strength that frightened ignorance can provide, to the emancipation of the proletariat; they see it as a horrible disgrace, as a catastrophe, as the end of civilization—when it is barely the beginning of it . . . simply because they do not understand their true interests, which are the same for every human entity." It would be impossible for one group to live at the expense of others and still achieve the goal of happiness and personal fulfillment. Satisfaction, he thought, could never be achieved by destroying the happiness of others.

"Heredity, education, and the unequal circumstances in life will already have created profound moral and even physical differences between the bourgeoisie and the proletariat; but one natural law keeps them united in the same common tendency: their personal improvement. Therein lies the true interest of every human being." Guerrero suggested that once the bourgeoisie understood this principle, they would support the transformation of society the anarchists advocated. "Some people will have gained, along with their freedom, their full right to life; the others will have lost, along with their superfluousness, the fear of losing it all." But, he warned, "If false interests continue to exert a domineering influence over the minds of the bourgeois, and if a portion of the workers continue, as they have so far, their opposition through passivism or their betrayals against the cause of labor, the change will come about through violence, crushing the obstructionists of progress."[23]

In "The Purposes of the Revolution" he wrote: "'Why, if you want freedom, do you not kill the tyrant and thus avoid the horrors of a major fratricidal war? Why do you not murder the despot who oppresses the people and who has put a price on your head?'—I have been asked many times. Because I am not an enemy of the tyrant, I have replied; because if I were to kill the man, tyranny would still be left standing, and it is the latter I combat.... Tyranny is the logical result of a social disease, whose present remedy is the Revolution." Citing the inviolable laws of nature, Guerrero argued that "tyrannies, the most bloodthirsty and ferocious despotisms cannot break that law, because it has no loopholes." They grow from the environment and revolution is the means of changing that environment. "Tyrants do not just appear in nations through a phenomenon of self-generation. The universal law of determinism knows them to be at the back of the peoples. That same law, manifested in the powerful revolutionary transformation, will make them fall forever, asphyxiated like a fish deprived of its liquid environment."[24]

That same issue of *Regeneración*, September 17, 1910, also carried two of Guerrero's poetic pieces, "Blow" and "I Am Action." In the first a tired, old vagabond flees the city and all its problems for the peace and solitude of the mountains. But a light breeze comes to haunt him with tales of its "long pilgrimage" through all the ills of society. "Go away, light breeze," he says, "I want to be alone." But the breeze, leaving, also leaves him troubled with all the human anguish it had seen. Then, in strong gusts, came an intense and powerful wind. "Who are you? Where do you come from?" the vagabond asks. The wind answers, "I come from all the corners of the world; I bring the just future; I am the wind of the revolution." He concluded:

> Blow, hurricane; comb my long hair with your terrible fingers. Blow, gale wind, blow over my steep rock, over the valleys, the abysses, turn around from the mountains; demolish those troop quarters and temples; destroy those prisons; shake that resignation; dissolve those clouds of incense; break the branches of the trees from which the oppressors made their lyres; awake them from that ignorance; pull up the gilding which represents a thousand miseries. Blow, hurricane, whirlwind, north wind, blow; lift the passive sands trampled by camels and the bellies of snakes and make them burning missiles. Blow, blow, and when the

Above, the staff of Regeneración, 1910. From left: Anselmo L. Figueroa, Guerrero, Ricardo Flores Magón, Enrique Flores Magón, and Librado Rivera. Guerrero's likeness was obvioulsy added to the photograph. (Author's collection.)

At right, Regeneración, September 3, 1910. The editors proclaimed the ideals of anarchism.

breeze returns it cannot leave the horrible anguish of human salvery imprisoned in my long hair.[25]

"I Am Action" was not nearly so dramatic, but the point was one that Guerrero made over and over about the need to follow words with deeds. "Without me, all the aspirations and ideals would roll around in the minds of men like dry leaves whirled about by the north wind. Progress and Liberty are not possible without me. I am Action."[26] Just months after the publishing of this essay Práxedis was dead.

In late September, Guerrero continued what had essentially become instructions in libertarian thought with "The Inconvenience of Gratitude." Explaining how "abuses of the powerful, the misery of people, the injustices . . . hunger and the exploitation . . . knock, day after day, on the door of a strong and fair man," the piece can be described as autobiographical. A man whose "dreams of freedom become highly passionate desires" sees his "energies turning idealism into action" and he becomes a "warrior, apostle or philospher," or maybe all three. He then "fights, he battles, he struggles, with the strength of brain and fist, until he perishes or he conquers." If he dies, he is forgotten or, perhaps, placed on the "ridiculous pedestal of idols." If he triumphs, however, "the admiration and the gratefulness of the crowds" will corrupt him, turning him into "a glorious tyrant." Guerrero affirmed: "the gratitude of the people is the most prolific creator of despotisms. It corrupts good men and it opens the road to power to the ambitious ones."

Developing these points at length, Guerrero argued that whether the hero or liberator was motivated by sincere aspirations for justice or was driven by utilitarian opportunism, "the gratitude of the people is unjustified." It may well be that the actions "are deserving of esteem, but not of gratitude. Gratitude is born from the false assumption, which is also the origin of the iniquitous authoritarian justice: the assumption of the free will of individuals . . . [gratitude] often makes nations pay for an imaginary freedom with the loss of their true rights and freedoms." Finally, Práxedis wrote: "The people do not owe any gratitude to their liberators, any more than they owe love to their tyrants."[27]

In the September 1910 issues of *Regeneración*, where he published his "Puntos Rojos" column, Guerrero's accounts of the revolutionary actions of 1908 appeared. In the inaugural issue his "The Death of the Heroes" described the results of those revolts for many of the participants who had been apprehended. He related the circumstances of the execution of José Lugo, one of the leaders of the uprising in Viesca, Coahuila, who died bravely and defiantly. Although they had not been directly connected with the *magonista* movement, Guerrero also described the trials and executions of three rebels against the Porfiriato in the Yucatán. "Ah! If Lugos, if Albertos, Ramírez Bonilla and Kankum do not affect the conscience of Mexicans," he angrily ended, "I will reject those people with the disdain of my saliva."[28]

His descriptions of the "Revolutionary Episodes" of "Las Vacas," "Viesca," and "Palomas" followed in the next three issues. The account of Las Vacas was so detailed that some thought that Guerrero had participated. The leader, former Mexican army officer, Encarnación Díaz Guerra, filed a complete report with the *PLM* leadership, and Práxedis had an opportunity to talk with many of the veterans of Las Vacas. What happened in Viesca, near the major city of Torreón (which was further removed from the border so that survivors had little opportunity to flee to the United States) was described in less detail. In the case of Palomas, Guerrero had, of course, led the attack.[29]

September 1910, the month *Regeneración* resumed publication was also the centennial of the *grito de Dolores*, Mexico's independence celebration, about which Guerrero expressed his concerns a year earlier in *Punto Rojo*. The centennial was celebrated elaborately and expensively in Mexico, with the government consciously turning it into a glorification of the peace and development identified with Porfirio Díaz and his regime. Elections had been held in the summer and Díaz declared the winner, but discontent from the supporters of the losing candidate, Francisco I. Madero, continued, and, as always, the *magonistas* doggedly persisted in their agitation. Consequently, the Mexican government zealously made certain nothing embarrasssing or riotous occurred during the observances of the centennial. This led to brutal actions and reactions in several parts of the Republic. Guerrero, in early October, commented bitterly about the situation in "Sweet Peace," noting, "The Mexican Press speaks of bloody events that took place during the celebration of the Centennial." Mentioning several specific incidents, Práxedis was particularly wrought over attacks on women and children.

> Mexico is no longer the portion of land bordered by the Bravo and Suchate rivers; it is the Company of the Borgias, dug out and turned into reddish foul-smelling quagmires. Mexico has had brutal tyrants who have sold its territories; who have have executed the philosophers and thinkers in times of war; who have sacrificed the doctors and the wounded in hospitals; who have stolen, incarcerated, killed without restraint, but none have, as does the current despotism, been characterized as executors of children and women.

Of the centennial observances, he wrote:

> The priests of the Subservient Peace stretched out their hands over the masses, and they made their foreheads vile with the dust of submission, and their knees, shaking with cowardice, they placed on the ground, prostituted with crime . . . the chant of the new liturgies is a combination of sinister noises, tied to each other at the end of their echoes;

the prayer, the lament, the whistling of the whip, the crunching of bones tortured by the shoes of the horses, the squeaking of doors in the prisons, the damnation of the hired assassin, the falling of bodies into the waters of the sea, the crackling of the settlements set on fire, the cautious steps of the spy, the whispering of the informant, the laughter of the courtesan, the clamor of adulation, the crying of the little ones, and the monotonous whisper of stupid prayers....

Sweet peace, divine peace. Let us love peace. Let us keep the peace of tranquility, at the cost of the dearest loved ones, even of life itself.... Children and women perished in Sonora; children and women have died in Veracruz and Tlaxcala; children and women, their backs bloody, their faces saddened, their limbs feeble, live as slaves in Yucatán and the Islas Marías, and ... we have peace, sweet peace, divine peace, paid for with the martyrdom of the people whom we should defend with our lives that shame us in this slavery.[30]

In his last years Guerrero became a strong advocate of the educational ideas of the Spaniard Francisco Ferrer y Guardia, libertarian writer and educator. Ferrer, intensely anti-religious, spent years in France in the late-nineteenth century and came in contact with the leading anarchist thinkers. While denying he was an anarchist, his *Escuela Moderna*, which he founded in Barcelona in 1901, emphasized a rational, scientific education as a prerequisite for social reform, just as the anarchists advocated. Ferrer was not an original thinker, but unlike the leading anarchists, he acquired substantial funds to support the implementation of his ideas. His *Escuela Moderna* served as a model for the modern school movement that had considerable influence in both the United States and Europe.

What projected Ferrer into international prominence and gained adherents for his educational ideas, was his martyrdom more than his educational reforms. In the summer of 1909 a social uprising—apparently spontaneous—in Barcelona became known as the *Semana Trágica*. Two years earlier Ferrer had been arrested and held a year before being acquitted on charges growing out of another attempted revolt. He was again arrested and charged before a court-martial by a repressive Spanish government. Although there was no evidence against him Ferrer was convicted and executed by a firing squad on October 13, 1909, at the Montjuich fortress. His last words reportedly concluded with, "I am innocent. Long live the Modern School." The Ferrer case provoked an international outcry, not to be matched in anarchist circles until the Sacco and Vanzetti case in the Untied States about two decades later.[31]

When Guerrero first came into contact with Ferrer's thinking is not clear, but by 1910 he was a strong advocate of the Modern School approach to educational reform. In "Let's Push Rational Education" in *Regeneración* of October 1, 1910, he wrote: "Soon it will be one year since the death of Francisco Ferrer, assassinated inside the fort of Montjuich . . . by the enemies of civilization." Guerrero wrote that he channeled his desire to cry out in protest against such action into the positive step of trying to establish schools and libraries on Ferrer's rationalist model among groups of Mexican workers. Lack of funds, books, and teachers had hampered the movement. Now as the anniversary of the execution approached, instead of protests, demonstrations, and acts of sympathy, Guerrero called for efforts to implement modern schools. "That would be the best protest, the most logical, the most conscious, the most effective," wrote Práxedis, adding, "There is no need of cries, or threats, simply action, immediate and constant action which will reach the heart of the despotism and which will be the healthy poison that will shorten its days."

Guerrero pointed out that workers' groups in the United States supported efforts to establish schools on the Ferrer model, but they, too, were hampered by lack of funds. He urged that workers from both the United States and Mexico agree to work toward a common goal:

> That our affection for Ferrer not degenerate into lyricism and idolatrous fantasies; his work will be in the hands of those who love liberty; and by continuing it, we protest against his executioners and we wound directly despotism.
> Let our children have the intellectual bread that invigorates the brain, not the indigestible food that debilitates them.
> Free education will assure the victories which comprise the armed revolution.
> Let's convert into fulfilled prophecy the last exclamation of the martyr of Montjuich. Let's make the Modern School live.[32]

Modern schools for Mexican children in the United States and Mexico were goals for the future. In October 1910 the likelihood of stronger movements to overthrow Díaz raised more immediate possibilities, and Guerrero faced new issues arising from the opportunities. With more revolutionary movements emerging, the fear of United States intervention in Mexico also increased. In "The Argument of Filogonio," Guerrero recounted the story of Filogonio and his companions, capsized in a boat in a rapidly flowing river, and how they reacted to the danger. When those who could swim fought to get to the shore, assisting others who could not, Filogonio denounced the efforts:

> You imbeciles! What are you doing? You imprudent ones! Can't you see that, with such an effort and such strokes, we can all die of exhaustion? We fell into this current because of one of us; the wise thing to do now, is to condemn it and to protest against it and not just keep making all those movements, because we might just happen to die of exhaustion, which is the worst way to die.

It was precisely Filogonio's argument of that Guerrero thought otherwise intelligent people used to oppose a revolution out of fear that it would bring United States intervention.

> People are saying, some with bad intentions and others out of ignorance, that the United States is waiting for a revolutionary movement in Mexico to intervene, to send its squads and its troops and to declare the annexation by any means. And they advise us to preserve the peace at all costs, even the very cost of slavery, in order not to give the powerful and almighty Government of Washington a chance to declare us a yankee province.

Guerrero used his own experiences in the United States to argue that the United States was totally opposed to revolution in Mexico. As long as the advocates of revolution were calling for economic and social reform, the United States, to protect the interests of its citizens, would oppose.

To those using the arguments of Filogonio, Guerrero addressed his by now usual denunciations of passivity: "Flocks of sheep do not command respect from anyone. . . . A passive people is slavery, honey on the corn flakes for the ambitious exploiters." But a people "rebelling for their liberty and rights becomes feared by the conquerors. . . . Let us leave Filogonio and the prudent to argue about the dangers of fatigue," he concluded. "Let us swim in order to come out of the current."[33]

Three weeks later Práxedis returned to this topic in "The Probable Intervention." While still contending that the United States, both government and capitalists, wanted to prevent revolution, the possibility was growing that the Mexican oligarchs, whether headed by Díaz or others, might provoke intervention to try to save themselves. If so, Guerrero predicted, the oligarchy would collapse. The Mexican people, including the army and the bourgeoisie, would unite to reject the conquest. It would not be a war of great battles, but guerrilla warfare, "the supreme weapon of oppressed nations, with which the invisible force of the oppressed can destroy day by day, year by year, the arrogant force of the military masses."

Mexico would present an incomparably worse battleground for the United States than the Philippines, where in 1910 American intervention was still newsworthy. Guerrero warned, the "Mexican shoe is very narrow for the foot of yankee imperialism." If the imperialists tried to wear it through intervention, soon they would be "pitifully limping, stumbling along not in the grand marches of triumphal ambition, but in shame of the failure of inglorius efforts, dragging along the nation." The revolution was coming, he wrote, interventionist threat or not, and he called on lovers of justice to stop intervention in any form, whether "it was favorable to the tyranny or to the Mexican people," because in either case it will be a "stupidity of tragic results."[34]

As the outbreak of hostilities neared, Guerrero continued to write on diverse topics. In "Working" he compared the hard life of the rural peasant, the miner, the woman textile worker, and the prostitute to the ease of the captain of industry, the judge protecting the despots, the henchman undermining the revolutionary, and the priest deceiving the people. The work of the revolutionary, Práxedis wrote, is to expose these evils through the written word, to bring on the revolution to allow the peasant, the miner, and the seamstress, a better life. In a society where all are equal neither the prostitute nor the priest would exist anymore. Though Guerrero wrote movingly of the revolutionary "working" by writing, his own impatience with the course of the revolt would soon take him from his desk and into the field against the Porfiriato.[35]

In "The Means and the End," published in early November 1910, he further explained the purpose of revolution, pointing out again that it was not the tyrant, Porfirio Díaz, who was the target of the revolt, but the system. As Guerrero himself drew closer to the decision to again take the field, he wrote of "the violence that unavoidably and necessarily has to accompany the liberation movement," saying "we deplore it and we find it disgusting, but in the alternative of continuing indefinitely enslaved, or appealing to the use of force, we choose the passing horrors of the armed struggle.... We are going to the violent struggle without making it into an ideal of ours . . ." he reiterated. "Our violence is not justice: it is simply a necessity fulfilled.... Our violence would have no purpose without the violence of the despotism. . . ." Having established the means, he once again clarified that "the end of revolutions . . . is to guarantee for everyone the right to life, destroying the causes of misery, of ignorance and despotism."[36]

In his last essays in *Regeneración*, Guerrero had addressed the issue of "Women."[37] Shortly before he left Los Angeles for the border, he published his incredulous reaction to the burning alive of Antonio Rodríguez in Rocksprings, Texas, in a piece entitled "Whites, Whites."[38] A number of other articles by Guerrero were published in *Regeneración* after his death, including "Revolutionary Women," as well as some of the work he had published for the Villarreal sisters under the pen name "Victoria Segura."[39]

Throughout his time with *Regeneración* in the fall 1910, Guerrero was also responsible for "Puntos Rojos," brief comments and aphorisms. In the anthologies of Guerrero's writings there are some noteworthy differences in the "Puntos Rojos." The collection put out by *Ediciones Antorcha*, entitled *Artículos de Combate*, reprinted the section from each issue of *Regeneración*. The collection edited by the *magonistas* in 1924, which was also used in Bartra's later collection on *Regeneración*, appears to be an edited version. One of the reasons for this difference, other than questions of space availability and editorial judgement, is that when Guerrero was writing these items, he commented on many topical issues that by 1924 were irrelevant or forgotten. Not having access to all the papers he wrote for makes it impossible to say with certainty when, where, and even if, he wrote all the items in the 1924 edition.

"It is better to die on your feet than to live on your knees," is an idea Práxedis lived and died by, and he may well have used it in *Punto Rojo* or one of the earlier papers, but that does not mean he originated the phrase anymore than Emiliano Zapata, with whom it is most identified in Mexico, did. It was not in the "Puntos Rojos" collected from the 1910 *Regeneración* but it was included in the 1924 work. It was not far removed from Guerrero's closing statement in "Boxer": "We are standing, we will kneel before no power." Indeed, many of his *puntos* were either ideas taken from some his longer pieces or ideas that developed into longer works. Some examples, most taken from the 1924 collection, which in some cases were shortened from the original forms:

> Sow a little seed of rebellion and you will determine a harvest of freedoms.
>
> Passivism and mildness do not imply kindness, any more than rebelliousness implies savagery.
>
> "We are hungry and thirsty for justice," can be heard everywhere; but how many of those hungry dare to take the bread, and how many of those thirsty risk to drink the water that is on the way to the revolution?
>
> If it seems to you that by walking, you won't reach freedom, then run.
>
> To live in order to be free, or to die in order to stop being slaves.
>
> For some sensitive spirits it is more painful and barbarian to see a thousand men die in the revolution than to see millions of men, women, and children live and die in the jails and in exploitation.
>
> The features of the tyrant represent a description of the people who obey him.

Who is more responsible: the tyrant who oppresses the people, or the people who created him?

If you feel the urge to bow down before a despot, go ahead, but pick up a rock to finish the salutation with dignity.

A cause does not succeed because of its kindness and its justice: it succeeds because of the efforts of its supporters.

There are many thieves in Mexico. There are people so degenerate that steal the insignificance of a piece of bread, when they could afford the luxury of starving to death. . . .[40]

Guerrero could not be content in the role of revolutionary writer as the Mexican Revolution began to finally develop in November 1910. Toward the end of the month he departed California for El Paso to organize forces to take into Mexico. By the end of the next month he was dead in Janos, Chihuahua. Ricardo Flores Magón, grief stricken by the loss, wrote:

And yet I cannot grasp the loss and give credence to the terrible reality. At any moment a hope hidden deep within my heart tells me that a comforting telegram will come saying that Práxedis is still among the living. The brutal truth cannot destroy in the deepest recesses of my heart a last remnant of hope like a flickering light ready to go out. And my tortured mind still hopes to meet him in his favorite haunts, in the office where we used to dream with him the dream of the dawn of social emancipation, and my restless eye seeks the martyr bent over his table of toil, writing, writing, writing.[41]

POET-REVOLUTIONARY

With his martyrdom at an early age made all the more tragic by his personal attractiveness, and with his well-known and seemingly selfless efforts for the cause of revolution during his last five years, an aura of romance surrounds Práxedis Guerrero. When his name comes up, which is not often, in both serious and popular discussions of the coming of the Mexican Revolution, it is easy to romanticize the "poet-revolutionary," the *"hacendado-peón."* The outline of his life is the stuff of legends: the hacendado's son forsaking a life of luxuries for the harshness of work in the copper and coal mines of the

American Southwest; the daring fugitive, relentlessly stalked by government and private agents of two nations, leaping out of third-story windows; the man on horseback, attempting to rally his meager forces by any means possible to strike a telling blow against the dictatorship.

Yet, Guerrero's importance to a full understanding of a rich and dramatic period in history of Mexico is undeniable— although largely unrecognized. In contrast, Ricardo Flores Magón remains controversial in Mexico today, even as he becomes more firmly entrenched in the pantheon of Mexican heroes. Historians debate the contributions of Flores Magón and the *magonistas* to the origins and development of the Mexican Revolution. Politicians invoke his name in the support of, or sometimes in opposition to, all manner of causes. Scholars from numerous countries study his deeds, measure his influence, and evaluate his writings. Few note, or seem to realize, that the Flores Magón movement itself, for almost three years—three very decisive years—was directed by Práxedis Guerrero. From 1907 to 1910 Guerrero roamed the borderlands from California to Texas organizing, arming, encouraging, and physically leading *magonistas* into battle. One might question whether there would have been a Flores Magón movement without Guerrero's efforts.

Guerrero's geographical range is important as well. His activities in all areas of the Southwest brought him into contact with the Mexican population along the United States-Mexico border. In trying to alter the course of Mexican history Guerrero became an actor in Mexican American history. In his relations with the Mexicans in the United States he demonstrated both the diversity of the population and the broad spectrum of his appeal. Copper miners in Arizona, railroad workers and coal miners in Texas, merchants and journalists, men and women, radicals of all stripes, and intellectuals in general responded positively to the young revolutionary. They were willing to support his efforts and even to follow him into battle. The interplay between

Guerrero and the Mexican population in the United States borderlands also substantiates the story of Mexican Americans defending their rights—a story being documented by historians like Juan Gómez Quiñones and Emilio Zamora.[1] Guerrero also concerned himself with issues and concerns unique to Mexicans in the United States, and his contributions to Mexican American history have been slighted even more than those he made to the country of his birth.

Studies of Mexican intellectual history, a neglected area in general, have also tended to overlook Guerrero. With the hectic pace of his life, his writings were often done on the run—and at times show the haste of preparation. His anarchist writings were not the product of original thought, but demonstrated careful reading and serious study. Many were skillful and imaginative presentations synthesizing the ideas of international anarchist theorists. His calls for action were many times moving and inspiring. His letters reflect a sensitive spirit as well as a sharp intellect. Flores Magón, recognized for years primarily as the "precursor" of the Mexican Revolution, has come to be appreciated as a multi-faceted individual. Serious studies of his thought and his writings continue. Guerrero merits some of that attention.

The Mexican Revolution produced a great number of men of action of the first rank. It produced fewer thinkers of prominence. National leaders such as Francisco I. Madero, Venustiano Carranza, Pancho Villa, Emiliano Zapata, Alvaro Obregón, and others of lesser stature, often were identified with one faction or another, but rarely considered to have a clearly defined intellectual position. Biographers and historians of the Revolution are still interpreting both the men and their movements. The intellectuals who were themselves active in the revolutionary epoch advised the leaders, but rarely had power to implement their ideas. Ricardo Flores Magón, Antonio Díaz Soto y Gama, Luis Cabrera, José Vasconcelos, Martín Luis Guzmán, and others wrote about revolution, in some cases influenced revolutionary actions, and no doubt aspired to even greater active roles.

None, however, seemed to combine "thinking" and "doing" to the extent that Práxedis Guerrero did. It is intriguing to speculate on the role Guerrero might have played in the epic decade of the Mexican Revolution. How much success could anarchism survive? What kind of sparks would fly from confrontations or collaborations of Guerrero and Villa, or Guerrero and Zapata, or Guerrero, the anarchist-idealist, and Obregón, the practical realist? Instead, we must be content with the conclusions of this study. Práxedis G. Guerrero was a major figure in the development of the movement led by Flores Magón—a movement that was instrumental in bringing on the Mexican Revolution in 1910. The anarchist Guerrero was a brilliant organizer, a prolific writer, and a brave fighter—he was a true revolutionary. Whatever else he might have become was snuffed out when he "died on his feet" at Janos, Chihuahua, in 1910. He would have never "lived on his knees."

"TO DIE ON YOUR FEET": SELECTED WRITINGS OF PRÁXEDIS G. GUERRERO

Throughout this study practically all of the known writings of Práxedis G. Guerrero have been mentioned, discussed, paraphrased, or quoted from to one degree or another. In addition to the published writings, many of his letters have also been incorporated into the work. In a few cases, the entire text of an essay is included, such as "Whites, Whites" in Chapter Five, or the greater portion of a reading, such as "Listen" or "Anniversary" in Chapter Seven. In order to acquaint the reader with the work of Guerrero further, and to put his thoughts and ideas into context, a selection of translations of his writings follows.

"Make Way" is one of the first efforts using a theme Guerrero would return to time and again, the inevitable coming of the Revolution, most often presented in dramatic or apocalyptical form.

MAKE WAY!

Out of the cluster of clouds, that the hurricane whirls around to darken the skies, comes the flaming sword wielded by an invisible arm, and with dazzling zig-zags writes on the page roaring with black smoke, the words MAKE WAY! And as the shadow becomes darker, the sword glows even brighter.

Out of the squall of hatred that besieges us; out of the black bosom of the tempests that tyranny unleashes over our foreheads, comes the invulnerable sword of the Idea and writes with the lightning of the word, the very heart of darkness, pages of honor to inextinguishable cry: MAKE WAY!

We walk bravely toward the summit; we meet obstacles; the rocks can't stop us; if we find abysses cutting our march, we throw over them, as a bridge, the words, MAKE WAY!, and we go across. In the midst of sinister jungles of daggers, parting the underbrush; jumping from the fields to the factories; from the prison to the grave; from the schools to the barracks; scourging the miserable armies of traitors and spies; we march forward saying MAKE WAY! Our advance does not stop to consider the harsh walls that oppress our brothers; their indomitable spirit has broken the bolt and crossed the bodies of the guards; it has, with disdain, told the sentries: MAKE WAY! and at our side has followed the road to the future.

You pipe dreamers, thrown by criminal decadence to the summit of power, dullards, sleepwalkers, can't you feel the gestation of fire? The mountain will throw you into the abyss when you hear the roaring explosion of the cry: MAKE WAY!

From the bottom of the ancient trunk that holds the historic and dear heirlooms, one has been taken out: beautiful and delicate hands will gird it around the brave chest of the guerilla warrior: the red shirt, terror of all banners, which says to the praetorians: MAKE WAY!

The old saber of Ayutla and the Reform jumps impatiently in its rusty sheath . . . MAKE WAY! to the heroic weapons of the redeeming struggles.

We arrive with serene hearts to the doors of glorious death and we knock with the hilt of the steel, crying: MAKE WAY!

—*Revolución*, September 14, 1907

In the following article Guerrero explains how tyrants such as Díaz are simply products of the environment and a revolution must elimnate the environment that produces tyrants. He does not specifically assert that it is the state that should be eliminated, although the implication is there.

THE PURPOSE OF THE REVOLUTION

"Why, if you want freedom, do you not kill the tyrant and thus avoid the horrors of a major fratricidal war? Why do you not murder the despot who oppresses people and who has put a price on your head?"—I have been asked many times. Because I am not an enemy of the tyrant, I have replied; because if I were to kill the man, tyranny would still be left standing, and it is the latter I combat; because if I were to blindly hurl myself against him, I would be doing what a dog does, when it bites a rock, hurting itself, but not knowing nor understanding where the pain comes from.

Tyranny is the logical result of a social disease, whose present remedy is the Revolution, since the pacific resistance of the doctrine of Tolstoy would only produce in these times the annihilation of the few who might ever have understood or practiced its simplicity.

Inviolable laws of nature rule over all things and beings; cause is the creator of effect; the environment determines in an absolute manner the appearance and the qualities of the product; worms originate where there is putrid matter; wherever an organism may appear and develop, it proves that there have been and there are contributing elements for its formation and nourishment. However bloodthirsty and ferocious they may be, tyrannies and despotisms cannot break that law, because it has no loopholes. They exist, therefore, in a special environmental state that prevails around them and from which they are the result. If they offend, if they cause harm, if they obstruct, we must seek their annulment in the transformation of that morbid environment, and not in the simple murder of the tyrant. The isolated death of one man, be he tsar, sultan, dictator or president, is ineffective if one wishes to destroy tyranny. It would be like trying to dry up a swamp by, from time to time, killing the reptiles that are born in it.

If things were otherwise, nothing would be more practical or simple than to go to the individual and to destroy him. Modern science places in our hands powerful instruments that possess certain and terrible effectiveness, and which used one time and creating an insignificant number of victims, would achieve freedom for the people and the Revolution would have no excuse or purpose.

For most people, revolution and war have the same meaning: a mistake which, in the light of misplaced judgments, makes the last resort of the oppressed look like barbarity. War has the invariable characteristics of hatred and national or personal ambitions; it creates a relative benefit for an individual or a group, paid for with the blood and the sacrifice of the masses. Revolution is the abrupt upheaval of the human tendency toward improvement, when a fairly numerous part of humanity is subjected by violence to a state incompatible to its needs and aspirations. Wars can be fought against a man, but never a revolution; the first destroys, perpetuating injustices; the latter mixes, shakes, confuses, disrupts, and casts the purifying fire of new ideas—the old elements poisoned by prejudices and eaten away by moths—to produce, from the scalding pot of the catastrophe, a more benign environment for the development and expansion of all beings. Revolution is the flood that spills over the dryness of the dead countryside, spreading the mud of life that transforms the uncultivated land of forced peace, where only reptiles live, into fertile fields suitable for the splendid blooming of higher species.

Tyrants do not just appear in nations through a phenomenon of self-generation. The universal law of determinism lifts them on the backs of the people. The same law, manifested in the powerful revolutionary transformation, will make them fall forever, asphyxiated, like a fish deprived of its liquid environment.

Revolution is a fully conscious act, it is not the spasm of a primitive bestiality. There is no lack of just inference between the guiding idea and the action set upon.

—*Regeneración*, September 17, 1910

> In the following piece, Guerrero argues that every individual seeks personal improvement, which cannot be achieved at the expense of anyone else. Completely redoing the structure of society is the only way this can be achieved, and it will have to be done by revolutionary change unless the bourgeoisie accept this fact. Again, Guerrero's reading of the leading anarchist theorists is evident in his analysis of the nature of society.

THE TRUE INTEREST OF THE BOURGEOISIE AND THE PROLETARIAT

Looking for happiness, many individuals spend their time devoting their efforts to the defense of false interests, moving away from the objective point of all their zeal and aspirations: personal improvement, and converting their struggle for life into a ferocious battle against their fellow man.

The privileged are opposed, with all the strength that frightened ignorance can provide, to the emancipation of the proletariat; they see it as a horrible disgrace, as a catastrophe, as the end of civilization—when it is barely the beginning of it—as a danger that must be combated by fire and sword, with all the weapons of cunning and violence, and they oppose it simply because they do not understand their true interests, which are the same for every human entity.

Stealing the bread from others means placing one's own sustenance in certain danger. Snatching the happiness of others means chaining oneself. Destroying other people's happiness in order to fabricate our own from its remains is nonsense. Because to attempt to raise one's own happiness over the misery and the grief of others is comparable to wanting to fortify a building by destroying its foundation. Nevertheless, most of the people, deceived by the appearance of their false interests, walk through the world like that, in search of their welfare under the banner of this absurd principle: to harm in order to benefit.

The particular interests of individuals, as well as those of the collective majority, lie in the complete satisfaction of their moral and physical needs, in the enjoyment of life, without threats or burdens that may embitter them. Those that oppose them, by breaking the ties of solidarity that nature established between members of the species, are working against themselves; since hurting others makes one's own welfare, which cannot be everlasting or certain, impossible: in the midst of a society that sleeps on thorns; of a society where hunger parades its pale face in front of full shops; where a portion of the men, who work themselves to exhaustion, can barely clothe or feed themselves; where the other portion of them snatch whatever comes out of their hands and their minds only to give to the moth and to useless monopoly; in an unbalanced society where both wealth and misery abound; where the concept of justice has such an iniquitous interpretation that many barbaric institutions are maintained for the sole purpose of persecuting and torturing the innocent victims of the aberrations that exist around them.

Heredity, education, and the unequal circumstances in life will already have created profound moral and even physical differences between the bourgeoisie and the proletariat; but one natural law keeps them united in the same common tendency: their personal improvement. There lies the true interest of every human being. And knowing that, makes it imperative to act rationally, by overcoming class prejudice and turning one's back on romanticism. Neither Charity, nor Humanitarianism, nor Self-sacrifice, have quite enough power to emancipate humanity, as does conscious Egoism.

There, where the bourgeois may be wise enough to understand it, the transformation of the present system is unavoidable and it would best serve their interests to facilitate that transformation, rather than to oppose it with stubborn resistance; the social problem that is currently shaking every corner of the world will lose its aspect of tragedy and will gently be resolved for the benefit of everyone. Some will have gained, along with their freedom, their full right to life; the others will have lost, along with their superfluousness, the fear of losing its all. And undoubtedly, the privileged of today will be the ones to benefit the most, in general terms. And that should put them to shame, since they are incapable of serving themselves; some of them need a slave to help them even to eat and to sleep. When the slave will no longer be there, they will have to acquire different habits, which will turn them into useful and active beings, capable of uniting their impulses to the collective effort that will then be applied to the harsh roughness of nature, and no longer to the stupid fight of man against man.

But if false interests continue to exert a domineering influence over the minds of the bourgeois, and if a portion of the workers continue, as they have so far, their opposition through passivism or their betrayals against the cause of labor, the change will come through violence, crushing the obstructionists of progress.

—*Regeneración*, September 10, 1910

Guerrero defends the use of violence in this article, but makes clear that it is not violence inspired by hatred, but a violence that is necessary to destroy the causes of tyranny in order to permit the development of the just society.

THE MEANS AND THE END

Tyrants and common criminals alike are subjected to the natural law of determinism, and, although their actions may horrify us or infuriate us, we must fairly agree upon the irresponsibility of both; but without arriving at absolute considerations, one could say that tyranny is the most forgivable of the crimes, because no person can commit it unless very complex circumstances coincide with it, circumstances beyond the will and out of the control of even the man most capable and endowed with qualities for evil. In fact, could there exist a tyrant over a people who did not provide him with the elements to sustain himself? A common wrongdoer can commit his misdeeds without the complicity of his victims; a despot cannot live or tyrannize without the cooperation of his, or a numerous part of them. Tyranny is the crime of the unconscious collectivities against themselves and must be attacked as a social disease by means of the Revolution, considering the death of the tyrants as an unavoidable incident of the struggle, an incident, and nothing more, but not an act of justice.

The two weights and the two measures have no use in libertarian standards. Science, by denying the free will of the enemy, destroys the basis of the present barbaric penal institutions; revolutionaries do not establish different criteria for the acts of a bigger or a smaller wrongdoer, nor do we have to seek evasive answers, to glaze over the violence that unavoidably and necessarily has to accompany the liberation movement. We deplore it and we find it disgusting, but in the alternative of continuing indefinitely enslaved, or appealing to the use of force, we choose the passing horrors of the armed struggle, without hatred toward the irresponsible tyrant, whose head will not roll to the ground just because justice demands it, but because the consequences of the long-lived despotism suffered by the people and the necessities of the moment will impose it, and when the time comes, in which the broken fences of passivism give way sincerely to the desires of freedom, exasperated by the confinement they have suffered, by the difficulties that have always had to be manifested.

We are going to the violent struggle without making it into an ideal of ours, without dreaming about the execution of the tyrants as the ultimate victory of justice.

Our violence is not justice, it is simply a necessity fulfilled in spite of emotions and idealisms, which alone are insufficient to guarantee a conquest of progress in the lives of people. Our violence would have no purpose without the violence of the despotism; nor could it be explained if the majority of the victims of the tyrant were neither conscious nor unconscious accomplices of the unjust present system, if the evolutionary power of human aspirations could find an unrestricted stage to extend itself in the social environment, the production of violence and its practice would be nonsensical; but this is now the practical environment to break old molds which the evolution of passivism would take centuries to gnaw.

The end to all revolutions, as we have said many times, is to guarantee for everyone the right to life, destroying the causes of misery, of ignorance, and of despotism; disdaining the uproar of sentimentality of the theoretical humanitarians.

—*Regeneración*, November 5, 1910

In the following piece, Guerrero discusses the relations between Mexico and the United States, responding to those who warned that revolution would bring United States intervention. In his appeal to socialism to defend against the capitalism of the United States, Guerrero uses the tactics of Flores Magón to attempt to obtain as much support as possible.

THE ARGUMENT OF FILOGONIO

As they were crossing a river, Filogonio and his friends capsized in their boat; some of them knew how to swim and tried to make it to the edge, while pulling out the ones who, from fear or inability to swim, were letting themselves be dragged by the current. Filogonio was able to stay afloat during a few minutes, but he did not swim toward the shore, nor did he pull anybody; he just spoke in the name of wisdom and common welfare, to those who were fighting for their lives against the waters.

"You imbeciles! What are you doing? Imprudent ones! Can't you see that with such an effort and such strokes, we can all die of exhaustion? We fell into this current because of one of us, now the wise thing to do is to condemn it and to protest against it and not to keep making all those movements, because we might just happen to die of exhaustion, which is the worst way to die."

So, Filogonio, yelling louder all the time, annoying those who were fighting to reach the edge, slowly kept getting away, dragged by the river. He was disappearing between the waves while taking big gulps of water, and each time he came up to the surface, he exclaimed again: "You imbeciles! You are going to die of exhaustion."

The story seems incredible. Nevertheless, out there in the world, some skillful and wise patriots are going around using Filogonio's argument, without appearing to be crazy, but rather seeming to be very intelligent and sane characters.

The threat of the North, the North American danger, has been, and is for many people the biggest patriotic reason to oppose the revolution. The fear of absorption by the Yankees, exploited by the Dictatorship and exploited by certain elements of the platonic opposition and of the "compromising" apostolate, has made the Mexican people forget, in part, the real danger into which the Government dealers have placed them.

During the violent Porfirian peace, both the larger and the smaller interests of Mexico have fallen into the threatening current of Yankee capitalism: natural resources, mines, forests, land, fisheries; and quickly the dependency on the financiers of the United States has been national reality in the political and the economic order. The will of the Yankee multimillionaires is, at the present time, the most powerful factor in the Mexican status quo. This is known by the Mexicans and also known by the foreigners. Peace in Mexico, as it stands today, constitutes the most favorable atmosphere for its complete absorption by the ambitious tendencies of the imperialism of the North, which works to preserve the peace, as it is understood that, if a Revolution does not completely snatch the prey from its hands, it will at least diminish the preponderant position of the United States, and the probabilities of absolute domination that it now holds for the future of Mexico.

People are saying, some with bad intentions and others out of ignorance, that the United States is waiting for a revolutionary movement in Mexico to intervene, to send its squads and troops and to declare the annexation by any means. And they advise us to preserve the peace at any cost, even the very cost of slavery, in order not to give the powerful and almighty Government of Washington a chance to declare us a Yankee province.

This is a childish argument, as childish as is the advice. The Government of the United States, which is both an instrument and servant of capitalism, is not waiting for, nor wants a revolution in Mexico; on the contrary, they fear it. All their actions have clearly demonstrated it. In violation of even the most trivial principles of justice, the Yankee government has been working toward the annihilation of the Mexican revolutionaries, launching against them a fury unprecedented in their history, which is filled with acts of different compliance toward all the revolutionaries who have sought refuge in their territory and who have organized from within it many movements, successful and failed. This persecution has had incidents that reveal the particular interest that Yankee capitalism places in not allowing the present peace to be disturbed, an interest that is far from being the simple wish of draining to the last drop the meaning of international treaties in order to preserve the power of a despot friend, but rather, if the desperate effort of someone who fights his own enemies, of someone who feels they are trying to take away from him a treasure of which he thought he was the undisputed owner. Otherwise, the Government of Washington would not have knocked so often and so audaciously on the doors of discredit, nor would it have raised, with its violence and abuses, that great movement of indignation that triggered the investigation now being carried out in the Congress for the illumination of the crimes committed against the Mexican Liberals in the United States.

In the United States, as anywhere else, there are honorable people who oppose the imperialism of their Government, and the greed of capitalism which has been undermining the old republican freedoms. Socialism, a constantly growing force, expands over the prairies of the West. It climbs the slopes of the Rocky Mountains, it palpitates in the huge cities of the East, it penetrates the forests of the South, it takes a seat at the desk of intellectuality; it spreads in the mines, in the railroads, in the fields, in the factories, and it stands in front of capitalism to say: "You will not pass through here." Labor unions, more numerous and more radical each day, are gaining ground in their disputes with their employers; and, thanks to the work of, and persecutions of, the Mexican revolutionaries, they have opened their eyes to the Mexican question, to study the relationship that Mexican slavery and peonage have with their situation. Cheap labor over there is the great enemy of organized labor here. Yankee capitalism has to consider these two factors, socialism and unionism, adding them to the ever growing black problem, the pending settlement with Japan, the ferment for emancipation in the Philippines, the unrest of Spanish America, the growth of the civilizing idea that rejects wars of conquest, the resistence that a people in rebellion, in a vast, mountainous territory, would offer to armed domination; and so, wisely they try to prolong the existing peace, which allows them to use Mexico as a warehouse for cheap slaves and as an inexhaustible deposit of material resources.

Maybe if the Mexican revolution were commanded by someone ambitious, and it did not have, as it does, the powerful social and economic reform tendencies, Yankee capitalism, working through the government, could seize the opportunity of aiding the pretender in order to share with him the same privileges as with the old tyrant, who would weaken and be forced to disappear. But in any case, the attempt to conquer Mexico in fire and blood would be an adventure of bad results.

The United States does not want a revolution in Mexico; that has been plainly demonstrated by their conduct. The danger of absorption and conquest is not a future threat when the Mexican people may want to obtain their freedom by the only practical means, by means of a revolution. It is rather a present danger; it is the current that drags us and from which we will not come out by being passive; we are within it and we must swim, swim vigorously toward the bank, even if Filogonio yells at us, telling us we are going to die of exhaustion if we do.

Flocks of sheep do not command respect from anyone, only Don Quixote could see in them a squadron of combatants.

A passive people is slavery, it is honey on the corn flakes for the ambitious exploiters. A people who are revolutionary for their liberty and rights become feared by the conquerors.

Let's leave Filogonio and the prudent ones to argue about the dangers of exhaustion. Let us swim, in order to come out of the current.

—*Regeneración*, October 8, 1910

In "Working" Guerrero graphically personalizes the three great enemies of the anarchists—property, state, and church. In the last paragraph he discusses the work of the revolutionary writer which may be as close as he ever came to an autobiographical effort.

WORKING

Over the fallow land that reverberates to the rays of the sun, with his skin tanned by the inclemency of the outdoors, his feet and hands cracked, the peasant works; he comes and goes over the furrows; dawn finds him up, and when the night comes, he is still grasping the tools and he works, he works. What does he work for? To fill up the barns that are not his; to pile up sustenance that rots waiting for scarcity while the peasant and his family can barely eat; to acquire debts that tie him down to the feet of his master, debts that will burden generations of his descendants; to be able to vegetate for a few years and to produce serfs who, when he dies, will plow the fields that consumed his life, and to give some feminine toys to the bestiality of his exploiters.

Sweaty and panting in the humid bottom of the mine, a man struggles against the rocks while his life is caressed by death, which he resembles in the paleness of his face; he dynamites and he hammers; he works while rheumatism filters across his tissues and tuberculosis weaves its deadly arabesques in the whiteness of his suffocated lungs. He works, he works. What does he work for? So that a few conceited persons can put gold on their garments and in their rooms, to fill the vaults of some miserable misers; to exchange his flesh for few metallic disks, made from the rocks he has brought to the surface by the ton; to die young and to abandon his beloved children in misery.

In a ramshackle hovel, sitting on a humble chair, a woman sews; she has eaten poorly, but she sews without rest; when others go out for a walk, she sews; when others sleep, she sews; the day runs out, and she keeps sewing with the light from a lamp, and little by little, her chest caves in and her eyes need to be closer and closer to the poor lamp that steals her brightness, and her coughing becomes a companion for her late nights. Silks, beautiful and fine textiles, they pass under needle; she works, she works. What does she work for? So the lazy women, aristocratic ladies, can attend the tournament of ostentation and envy; to stock luxurious wardrobes, where the garments will mildew while she clothes her premature old age with rags.

Wrapped in flashy trimmings, loaded with pungent perfumes, her withered face dyed, and faking affectionate overtones, the prostitute stalks men in front of her door, which was damned by the very prudery that forced her to take the ephemeral charms of her body to the social market. That woman works, a horrible job she has, she always works, she works. What does she work for? To acquire dirty diseases; to pay the moralizing State a sin tax and to atone for other people's crimes in her world of repulsion and filth.

At a luxurious desk, the king of industry, the lord of capital, calculates; the figures are born in his brain, and new combinations, far from the opulent dwelling, go to diminish the heat of the home and the chunks of hard bread of the proletariat; he works, he works, he also works. What does he work for? To amass superfluity in his palaces and to worsen the misery in the shacks; to take away from those who fabricate his wealth the food and shelter that their hands produce; to keep the dispossessed from ever insuring their right, that nature gave everyone, to live; to make sure that a great part of humanity remains as a flock that becomes impoverished without protest and without danger.

The judge feverishly searches in the volumes that fill the shelves of his study; he checks books, he jots down chapters, he turns over files, he browses through lawsuits; he rummages through the statements of alleged criminals; he toughens the criminological inventiveness of his brain; he works, he works. What does he work for? So he can justify all social errors with a legal pretext; to kill the natural rights with his written rights; to make sure that the whims of the despots are respected and feared; to always present to the eyes of man the dreadful head of Medusa on the stage of justice.

The henchman goes by the doors, listening, his beady little eyes peeking through the cracks, he studies the faces trying to distingush the characteristic features of rebellion; his ears stretch trying to perceive all the noise that could be alarming to the despotism; he disguises himself, but he cannot hide; the henchman has his own particular smell that gives him away; he can just as quickly become a worm or a snake; he rattles, he sways, he slips through the crowds, trying to read thought; he sticks to the walls as if he wanted to suck out the secrets within them; he hits, he kills, he chains; he works, he works. What does he work for? So that the oppressors can have tranquility in their palaces, erected over misery and slavery; so that humanity cannot think, cannot right itself, nor march toward emancipation.

Pointing up to the sky with his evil finger and spelling out the pages of absurd books, the priest runs to the house of ignorance; he preaches charity and he gets rich from dispossession; he speaks lies in the name of truth, he prays and deceives; he works, he works. What does he work for? To stupefy people and to split the ownership of the lands with the despots.

And so, gloomy and pensive, the revolutionary meditates; he leans over any old piece of paper and he writes strong phrases that hurt, that shake, that vibrate like the bugles of a storm; he wanders and he ignites with the flames of his words, the extinguished consciences, he sows rebellion and discontent; he forges the weapons of freedom with iron from the chains that he destroys; restlessly, he goes through the crowds taking to them the ideas and the hopes; he works, he works. What does he work for? So that the peasant can enjoy the products of his care, and the miner, without sacrificing his life, can have plenty of bread; so that the seamstress can sew dresses for herself and can also enjoy the sweet things in life; so that love can be the feeling that, honoring and perpetuating the species, can join two free beings; so that neither the king of industry, nor the judge, nor the henchman spend their lives working in detriment of mankind; so that the priest and prostitute both disappear; so that tyranny, despotism and ignorance all die; so that justice and freedom, rationally making all human beings equal, can make them into the solidaristic builders of a common welfare; so that everyone has, without having to descend into degradation, an assured right to life.

—*Regeneración*, October 8, 1910

Of several writings on women the following is Guerrero's longest and most complete in terms of his thoughts, although indicating he had some uncertainties himself as to what libertarian and feminist ideas meant in the real world of relations between men and women.

WOMEN

Children and women have always been the chosen victims of barbarism, and only in a few countries have the latter enjoyed some privileges, which, on occasion, place her socially above men, like in the primitive clans where matriarchy existed. But women are yet to

Práxedis G. Guerrero, 1882-1910. (Author's collection.)

occupy the true place in most societies that, as women, they deserve.

The Bible, which consecrates the impurity of women, tells us how the Jewish people treated women and children without any consideration: fathers had an absolute right over their daughters; they sold them as slaves or they sacrificed them, as demonstrated by the renowned case of Jephtah and the atrocious cult of Molloch in all peoples of the Semitic race, who put into practice the burning of live children, especially little girls. The Jews practiced the monopoly of women by the rich. Solomon gives us an example of that, and because of this, the poor produced the repugnant vices the Bible describes, with its consequent lowering of customs, whose victims of preference were women.

In ancient Egypt, where the poor fellahs built, under the force of the whip and the stick, gigantic monuments to subservience and pride, which the erosion of winds has not been able to destroy in the course of thousands of years, a woman had extraordinary privileges: she freely stipulated the clauses of marriage contracts, she could obtain a divorce by simply expressing her desire not to continue united to her husband, and it was not unusual to force the latter to serve her; exactly like many husbands today, who call themselves civilized, demand the servitude of their wives.

The women in India, as opposed to the Egyptian women, suffered the tyranny of horrible customs: the widows would burn themselves alive upon the death of their husbands. They were not forced into sacrifice by means of violence: men found the way to lead them to the pyre voluntarily by instilling in them absurd notions of honor, and exploiting their vanity, their pride and lineage, because, we should know, only the women of rank burned themselves. The women of the poor, who belonged to castes considered inferior, shamed themselves with their children in degradation; their life did not offer anything attractive.

China is another of the most dreadful countries: paternal authority was, and is despotic there, as is the authority of the husband: "woman is nothing more than a shadow or echo in the home," says the proverb; a woman cannot manifest any preferences because the precepts of decency would be offended; she should consider herself happy with the husband that is assigned to her, young or old, repugnant or tolerable; marriage is simply a sale. The morbid sensuality of the Chinese goes so far as the mutilation of feminine feet, along with other refinements common among the rich. As in India, the practice of suicide by the widows existed in China, although without the simultaneous bonfire, and rewarding them with inscriptions of praise in the temples. Infanticide is commonplace, especially with girls.

The Greeks, in spite of their powerful mentality, were not very humane with their women; Aeschylus, poet and philosopher, defender of patriarchical institutions, arrived at the odd theory that the woman is not the mother of the child, but only a temporary repository for the child of man. The gynoecium was the place destined for Hellenic women, although they frequently trained in gymnasiums; at one time young women actually received special education for love, but they were never seen as men's equals. Marriage was not a matter of inclination; the most robust and beautiful young men were matched with the most shapely young girls, as is the case in the cattle ranches, for the improvement of the race. Children received a military education; in order to remain superior over their slaves and neighbors, the Greeks formed soldiers from the cradle, healthy of body, but mutilated of spirit since Greek intellect, brilliant in some facets, remained dark in many others, in spite of the exaggerated praises made about Athenian culture: killing children who were weak and deformed, exercising the others in wrestling, in running, in all kinds of physical games. They became good warriors, with agile bodies, with beautiful and elegant shapes; but with such a discipline they stopped the intellectual development of the race, which otherwise would have reached much higher and more resplendent heights.

A tribe in Madagascar, the Hovas, understand the situation and can serve as an example of good treatment of women to many of the peoples that are considered civilized. The Hovas refer to their neighbors, the black women of Senegal, who were militarily civilized by the French, as "mules" because these unhappy women live subjected to the hardest and most humiliating labor.

The slandered nomadic Bedouins possess features that do them credit; among them, a delinquent could escape punishment if he managed to place himself under the cloak of a woman while exclaiming: "I place myself under your protection."

Different, as one can see, have been the fortunes of women. Among the Jews, a woman was an impure and salable slave, the absolute property of the father. In Egypt, she could exercise tyranny over men; in India she was the appendix that had to disappear with her owner; in China, as a victim of the sensuality and the jealousy of men, she had, and continues to have a sad fortune; in Greece, she was considered, with a few exceptions, as an object; among the Hovas, the Bedouins and other tribes, she enjoyed a relative freedom and very sympathetic laws. Look at her now, in situations also very diverse, in modern nations.

The morality that ancient civilizations inherited from the first social nuclei, known by the name of clans, is being modified by the evolution of customs, with the disappearance of certain needs and the birth of others; but generally speaking, women remain far from their rightful place, and the children who receive from them the initial impulse of their physical life, will undertake, when they become men, to perpetuate disagreement between the two parts that comprise humanity. Nowadays, widows are no longer burned along with the bodies of their husbands, nor do fathers have the right of life and death over their children, as was the case with Rome; armed raids to provide the men of a tribe with women are no longer in practice, nor are children burned under the nose of Molloch anymore; now, written laws and simple social conveniences perform the role of torturers of women; paternal authority is still manifested in a thousand oppressive ways; "White slavery" to supply the harems of the potentates occupies the place of the violent raids, and infanticide, the result of misery and bigotry, is a well known fact in all social classes.

Outside the field of liberalism, which vindicates the equality of men and women, the tendency of the times, which is still too weak to do away with all the obstacles offered against the emancipation of women, has triggered that digression known as "feminism." Not being able to be a woman, a woman wants to be a man; she rushes forth with enthusiasm worthy of a more rational feminism, in search of all the ugly things that a man can be and do; she wants to perform the functions of a policeman, a shyster, a political tyrant and to choose, along with men, the masters of the human race. Finland is at the head of this movement, followed by England and the United States.

Feminism serves as the basis for their opposition for the enemies of the emancipation of women. Indeed, there is nothing attractive about a woman gendarme, about a woman removed from the sweet mission of her sex to brandish the whip of oppression; about a woman fleeing from her gracious feminine inindvidualiy to dress in the hybridity of "masculiness."

The biblical theory of the impurity of women has lost its infallibility; it is replaced by the modern "inferiority of women," with the pretended support of science.

Inferiority of women! When, to be sincere, we should say: slavery of women!

Countless generations have gone by which subjected women to the rigors of a purposeful education, and finally, when the results of that education began to manifest themselves; when the prejudices accumulated in the feminine brain and the coarse burdens that men put on them act as a ballast in their lives preventing the open flight of their intellect over the free space of ideas, when everything that surrounds them is oppressive and false, we arrive at the conclusion of the inferiority of women. So we do not have to admit or confess the inequality of circumstances and the absence of opportunities, which, in spite of everything, have not prevented the beginning of the emancipation of women, assisted by her own heroic efforts. The morally emancipated women victoriously answer the charges of superficiality made against their sex; they make us meditate with respectful empathy in the sum total of valor, energy, willpower, sacrifice, and anguish that their labor represents; it is the greatest merit their rebelliousness possesses, compared with the rebelliousness of men. The act of the Russian revolutionary woman who disfigured her own face because her beauty was an obstacle in the fight for freedom reveals a superior mentality. Compare that action to that of the soldiers of Pompeii, running away from the troops of Caesar who had instructions to hit them in the face; look at Maximilian of Austria who refused to flee because he did not want to shave off his beautiful beard. On whose side are superfluosness, stupid coquetry, and stubborn vanity? We criticize the fragility of women, but can those errors that moral hypocrisy condemns compare with the homosexual deviations, with the infamous male prostitution, so extensive in all countries of the world and practiced scandalously by representatives of the so-called cultured classes, among men of the State and the refined nobility as the irreverent pen of Maximillian Harden made known in Germany, as it was sensationally discovered in Mexico during an intimate aristocratic ball?

Religion, whatever denomination it may be, is the most terrible enemy of women. On the pretext of giving counsel, it destroys her conscience; in the name of a barren love, it snatches away a love full of human life and happiness; with illusionary supports sketched in sickly poetry, it removes strong, real, immense poetry of free existence.

Religion is the assistant of the despots, both foreign and domestic; its mission is that of the animal tamer; a caress or lash, a cage or a rope, everything he uses leads to one end: to tame, to enslave women in the first place, because a woman is the mother and the teacher of the child, and the child will one day be a man.

Women have another no less terrible enemy: established customs; those venerable customs of our elders, always broken by progress and tied up again by conservatism. A woman cannot live as a free companion of a man, because customs are opposed to it, because a violation of the customs brings contempt, jeering, insults, and damnation. Customs have sanctified her slavery, her eternal minority of age, and she must continue being a slave and a pupil out of respect for the customs; without remembering that the sacred customs of our forefathers included cannibalism, human sacrifices in the altars of the god Huizilopochtli, the burning of children and widows, the piercing of noses and lips, the adoration of lizards, sheep and elephants. The sanctified customs of yesteryear are the crimes or the childish nonsense of today. To what then, do we owe such respect and compliance of the customs that obstruct the emancipation of women.

Freedom scares those who do not understand it and those who have created their environments from the degradation and misery of other people; that is why the emancipation of women finds a hundred opponents for every man who defends her or works for her.

Libertarian equality does not attempt to turn a woman into a man; it gives the same opportunities to both factions of the human race, so that both can develop without obstacles, naturally benefiting from the mutual support, without snatching away each other's rights, without obstructing the place that each of them has in nature. We men and women must fight for that rational equality, the harmonizer of the individual happiness with the collective happiness, because without it there will perpetually exist in the homes a seed of tyranny, which is the sprout of slavery and social misfortune. If customs are a yoke, let us break the customs, however sacred they may seem; by offending customs, civilization advances. Customs may be a restraint; but restraints have never liberated people, satisfied hunger, nor redeemed slavery.

—*Regeneración*, November 12, 1910

Guerrero's accounts of the battles in the attempted revolution of 1908 were published under the general heading, "Revolutionary Episodes." The following recounts the episode he personally led.

PALOMAS

This chapter in the history of freedom should be called *Francisco*

Manrique; it should carry the name of that youth, almost a child, who died by the bullets of the tyranny on July 1, 1908, in the frontier village of Palomas. The facts outline his silhouette over the blurred background of that almost unknown journey, that vanishes in the gray panorama of the desert.

Barely eleven libertarians could be gathered when the persecutions fell as hail over the revolutionary fields. Eleven and not one more, to attempt, with an audacious move, to save the revolution which seemed to be shipwrecked in the surf of treachery and cowardice.

The red dawn had already broken over Las Vacas, and Viesca, evacuated by the revolution, still resounded with the subversive cry of our *bandits*, when this small group formed in the middle of the repressive violence, and hurled, with only a fistful of cartridges and a few bombs manufactured with substandard materials, against an enemy perched up to recieve them with countless elements of resistance, against a tyranny made stronger by the forces of stupidity, fear, and indifference, toward the secular despotism that sinks its heels into the disgraceful carpet of quiet backs called national passivism.

Palomas was in the path that the group was supposed to follow; its capture was not important for the development of the strategic plan adopted, but it was convenient to scare the *rurales* and the treasury guards who watched it, in order to cross the desert without being disturbed by the vigilance.

Along the way, the telegraph wires were cut at intervals.

With their carbines firmly grasped and ready to shoot, their sombreros pushed back, with cautious and yet firm steps, their ears attentive to every sound while their scowl concentrated its visual focus on the blackness of the night, the eleven men arrived to the proximities of the Customs Office. Two bombs thrown at it showed it to be empty. The *rurales* and the treasury guards, forcing the local men to take up arms, had taken refuge inside the barracks. Before the attack, the group checked the houses to make sure they did not leave any enemies at their backs, at the same time putting the women at ease by explaining to them, in brief phrases, the objectives of the revolution.

Soon the walls of the barracks were within their grasp, and soon, its loopholes and rooftops showed, with the flashes of the rifles, and the number of its defenders. There were inside twice as many or more men than outside. The battle began unevenly for the attacking group. The adobe walls were a magnificent defense against the bullets of the Winchester rifles, and the bombs that could have resolved the situation in a few seconds turned out to be too small.

Francisco Manrique, always the first in all dangers, advanced toward the door of the barracks, engaging in battle with his chest exposed, and when he was two steps away from the loopholes that were spitting fire and steel, he fell mortally wounded.

The battle continued, the bullets whistling from top to bottom and bottom to top. The horizon was getting paler with the proximity of the sunshine, and Pancho was getting paler too, invaded by death, which kept advancing over his formerly proud, agile, and daring body. The sun was rising, blending its brightness with that of a revolutionary star eclipsing.

It was necessary to continue the battle toward the heart of the mountains. It was imperative to spread the fires of the rebellion quickly to as many places as possible.

The last bomb was used to blow up a door and take a few horses.

Pancho, who had fainted, seemed dead.

The interest of the cause had sacrificed the life of an exceptional fighter, and that same interest cruelly imposed the abandonment of his body in front of those walls splattered with his blood, spectators of his agony, the witnesses of his last and beautiful act of sublime stoicism.

Pancho regained consciousness, shortly after the withdrawal of his ten companions. He was interrogated, and he had the serenity to answer everything, while trying with his words to indirectly help his friends. He remained incognito until his death, lucidly thinking that if his real name became known, the despotism, guessing who had accompanied him, would try to annihilate them if the revolution were defeated. They were unable to find out from him any plots or names, or anything that could have assisted the tyranny.

Pancho loved truth. He never lied to avoid a responsibility or obtain a benefit. His word was frank and loyal, sometimes rude, but always sincere. And he, who had always disdained the life and the welfare bought with falseness, died lying (a sublime lie), wrapped in the anonymity of a conventional name—Otilio Madrid—in order to save the revolution and his friends.

I knew Pancho since we were children. In school we shared the same bench. Later, in adolescence, we traveled together through exploitation and misery, and later still, our ideals and our efforts joined together in the revolution. We were brothers as few brothers can be. No one entered, like I did, the beauty of his intimacy: he was a deeply kind young man, in spite of having had a nature as brave as the sea during a storm.

Pancho quit the job he had in the Treasury of the State of Guanajuato, in order to become a blue collar worker and later a courageous champion of freedom, in whose name he sacrificed his exsistence, so full of intense storms and great grief, which he knew how to subdue with his will of diamond. The two great loves of his life were his kind and excellent mother and freedom. He lived in misery, suffering the exploitation and injustices by the bourgeoisie, because he never wanted to be a bourgeois or an exploiter. When his father died, he gave up his inheritance left him. Having had the opportunity to live off a government job, he became its enemy instead and fought against it from the heights of his voluntary and proud misery. He was a rebel of the moral makings of Bakunin: action and idealism amalgamated harmoniously within his brain. Anywhere the revolution needed his activity, he went there, whether or not there was any money, because he knew how to get ahead through his cleverness, his energy and his sacrifices.

That was Otilio Madrid, whom they called the *leader* of the *bandits* of Palomas. That was the man who lived for truth and expired wrapped in a sublime lie, in whose pale lips two names palpitated in the last minute: that of his dear mother and mine, the one of his brothers who still lives to do justice to his memory and to continue the struggle in which he shed his blood; who still lives to apostrophize the passivism of a people, with the heroic and youthful silhouette of the one sacrificed at Palomas. . . .

How many were the men of the government who died in combat? Tyranny has managed to keep it a secret.

Nature took the side of the despotism.

The group was defeated by the terrible Amazon of the desert: thirst; the flame that swelters, the serpent that chokes, the anxiety that drives one crazy; the voluptuous companion of those soft and restless dunes . . . neither the saber nor the rifle. . . . Thirst, with the indescribable grimace of its caress; roasting the lips with its kisses; horribly drying the tongue with its burning breath; furiously scratching at the throat, it stopped those atoms of rebellion . . . and, in the distance, there was a mirage of a crystalline lake, laughing at the thirsty men who kept dragging along, brandishing their carbines impotent to combat the Amazon beast of the desert, while furiously biting the ashen weeds, that offered neither shade nor juice.

—*Regeneración*, September 24, 1910

NOTES

1—The Early Years

1. This discussion of the regime of Porfirio Díaz is based on several general accounts. For some very recent interpretations see Colin M. MacLachan and William H. Beezley, *El Gran Pueblo: A History of Greater Mexico* (Englewood Cliffs, New Jersey: Prentice Hall, 1994) 78-195. A standard text for some years, Michael C. Meyer and William L. Sherman, *The Course of Mexican History*, fifth edition (New York: Oxford University Press, 1995) also has a good section on the Porfiriato, "The Modernization of Mexico, 1876-1910," 431-479. Another good survey is Friedrich Katz, "The Liberal Republic and the Porfiriato, 1867-1910," in Leslie Bethell, editor, *Mexico Since Independence* (Cambridge: Cambridge University Press, 1991), 49-124.

2. Practically the only source for the early life of Práxedis Guerrero is Eugenio Martínez Núñez, *La vida heroica de Práxedis G. Guerrero* (Mexico: Instituto Nacional de Estudios Históricos de la Revolución Mexicana, 1960). The work was written in 1935 and contains annotations by Enrique Flores Magón and an introduction by Antonio Díaz Soto y Gama. The account here follows Martínez Núñez in the general outlines. He had access to letters and journals which I have been unable to locate in the originals. Translations of specific information from such items are noted. The only other attempt at a biography is a work by the Italian scholar, Piero Ferrua, *Gli Anarchici Nella Rivoluzione Messicana: Práxedis G. Guerrero* (Ragusa: Edizione "La Fiasccola, 1976). Ferrua relies heavily on Martínez Núñez.

3. Pbro. Jesús Ibarra Grande, *Jaral de Berrio y su Marquesada* (León, Guanajuato, 1990).

4. In April 1994, I visited the ruins of Los Altos de Ibarra. Francisco Longoria, who was born and grew up on the hacienda, still lives in a portion of one of the old buildings and maintains a small store there. His father, too, had spent his entire life living there, having been a worker on the hacienda. Understandably reserved and hesitant to talk to me, when he realized I was there to learn what I could about Práxedis Guerrero, Longoria kindly gave me a tour of Los Altos de Ibarra, particularly the remains of the main house, now completely in ruin. Not only did he have his own memories, but he also told me stories of life at Los Altos de Ibarra as related by his father, who was contemporary with the brothers and sisters of Práxedis.

5. Martínez Núñez, *La vida heroica*, 27.

6. *Ibid.*

7. The physical description of Guerrero comes from an informer's report to a Mexican consul in the United States in 1910. The informer had known him in Morenci, Arizona, in 1906 and 1907. See Arturo M. Elías, Mexican Consul in Tucson, Arizona, to Secretaría de Relaciones Exteriores, February 11, 1910, in Archivo "Genaro Estrada" de Secretaría de Relaciones Exteriores, Mexico (cited hereafter as ARE), L-E-952. There are only two known photographs of Guerrero.

8. Martínez Núñez, *La vida heroica*, 28-29.

9. *Ibid.*, 30.

10. Carlos Arturo Navarro Valtierra, director of the Archivo Histórico Municipal in León, Guanajuato, has devoted considerable time to a study of Guerrero's life. He believes Guerrero must have been exposed to *PLM* ideas in San Luis Potosí. He also believes that Manrique was more significant in the intellectual development of Guerrero than credited.

11. On Reyes, the Liberals, and the suppressions, see James Cockcroft, *Intellectual Precursors of the Mexican Revolution, 1900-1913* (Austin: University of Texas Press, 1968), 62, 101, 112-113.

12. Martínez Núñez, *La vida heroica*, 36.

13. *Ibid.*, 36.

14. *Ibid.*, 37.

15. *Ibid.*, 40.

16. *Ibid.*

17. *Ibid.*, 41.

2 — The *Magonistas* Against The Porfiriato

1. See Ward S. Albro, *Always a Rebel: Ricardo Flores Magón and the Mexican Revolution* (Fort Worth: Texas Christian University Press, 1992). Most of this chapter is summarized from material in my earlier study of the Flores Magón movement. For the primary material on which it is based, consult that work. Also see Cockcroft, *Intellectual Precursors*; Salvador Hernández Padilla, *El Magonismo: Historia de una pasión libertaria, 1900-1922* (Mexico: Ediciones Era, 1984); Colin M. MacLachlan, *Anarchism and the Mexican Revolution: The Political Trials of Ricardo Flores Magón in the United States* (Berkeley: University of California Press, 1991); W. Dirk Raat, *Revoltosos: Mexico's Rebels in the United States, 1903-1923* (College Station: Texas A&M University Press, 1981).

2. Albro, *Always a Rebel*, 8-11; Cockcroft, *Intellectual Precursors*, 13-100.

3. Recently, letters written in the 1890s from the mother of Ricardo Flores Magón to Porfirio Díaz seeking government employment for her sons, espe-

cially Ricardo, have surfaced in the Colección Porfirio Díaz of the Universidad Iberoamericana in Mexico. It is intriguing to speculate on what effects some government sinecure might have had on not only the Mexican Revolution but also international anarchism. See *Nexos*, September 1993, 85.

4. Albro, *Always a Rebel*, 11-22; Martínez Núñez, *La vida heroica*, 33-34

5. Albro, *Always a Rebel*, 23-33.

6. Raat, *Revoltosos*, is the best source for documenting the infiltration of the *magonista* movement by both governmental and private agents. Two collections of government documents reveal how thorough that infiltration became: Records of the United States Department of Justice, Record Group 74, Files 90755 and 180187 in the National Archives in Washington, D.C. (cited hereafter as Justice) and the files on the *magonista* movement in the Archivo "Genaro Estrada" de Secretaría de Relaciones Exteriores in Mexico, Legajos 918 to 954. Thomas Furlong described his career in *Fifty Years a Detective* (St. Louis: C. E. Barnett, 1912).

7. On the Cananea strike, Raat (*Revoltosos*, 65-91), remains the most complete and convincing account; John Mason Hart, *Revolutionary Mexico: The Coming and Process of the Mexican Revolution* (Berkeley: University of California Press, 1987), 63-68, has an interesting interpretation. Also see Hernández Padilla, *El Magonismo*, 30-49. The constitution of Guerrero's group is found in *Práxedis G. Guerrero, Artículos de Combate* (Mexico: Ediciones Antorcha, 1984), 33.

8. Copies of the *Programa y Manifesto* are available in many sources. See, for example, *Los Hermanos Flores Magón: Manifesto del Partido Liberal Mexicano* (Mexico: Instituto Nacional de Estudios Históricos de la Revolución Mexicana, 1985), 19-50. For a discussion of the development of the document, see Albro, *Always a Rebel*, 44-56.

9. See Albro, *Always a Rebel*, 57-60, for a discussion of the events of 1906 based on U. S. Department of Justice records.

10. Guerrero was in Morenci, Arizona, working for a copper mining company. Although there were many Mexican workers in Morenci and nearby Clifton, and Guerrero's *Obreros Libres* affiliated with the PLM in June 1906, the Morenci-Clifton area is well over 100 miles from the border. The *magonista* hopes of starting a revolt in 1906 were concentrated in the immediate border area around Douglas, Arizona, and Agua Prieta, Sonora. Piero Ferrua speculates that Guerrero might have been on missions in Mexico for the junta in the fall of 1906 and early 1907, but this is unlikely. See *Gli Anarchici*, 96-97.

11. Albro, *Always a Rebel*, 60-62. Aguirre is an interesting character. He had earlier been involved with the millenarian movement associated with Teresa Urrea, the Saint of Cabora, in Chihuahua and Arizona. He moved to El Paso in the 1890s, taught school, published his newspaper, and provided the presses

for numerous other papers, including *La Voz de la Mujer*. A constant critic of the Porfiriato, Aguirre came to be seen as something of a "revolutionary crank." Although helpful on many occasions, he was never as involved with the *magonista* movement as Mexican and U. S. authorities believed. See Raat, *Revoltosos*, 33, 95-96.

12. Text of proclamation in *Los Hermanos Florés Magón*, 105-107.

13. Albro, *Always a Rebel*, 62-63.

14. Cándido Donato Padua, *Movimiento revolucionario 1906 en Veracruz*, 2nd ed. (Tlalpán, D. F.: n.p. 1941), 21-25.

15. Albro, *Always a Rebel*, 64-66. For some of the reaction in St. Louis, see *St. Louis Post Dispatch* and *St. Louis Republic*, both November 20, 1906, editions.

16. Albro, *Always a Rebel*, 66-71; Raat, *Revoltosos*, 132-136.

17. Albro, *Always a Rebel*, 71-72, 78-79.

18. *Ibid.*, 80.

19. On the kidnapping, see Ward S. Albro, "El secuestro de Manuel Sarabia," *Historia Mexicana*, 18 (Jan.-March 1969), 400-407; Manuel Sarabia, "How I Was Kidnapped," *The Border*, Vol. I, No. 2 (Dec. 1908), 1-4; Raat, *Revoltosos*, 46-48, 53, 118, 142-146, 185; [Douglas, Arizona] *International-American*, July 13, 1907.

20. Albro, *Always a Rebel*, 84-85; *San Francisco Call*, August 10, 1907.

3—On Becoming A Revolutionary

1. Guerrero later reflected that his meeting with Sarabia was what led him into the movement. See letter from Guerrero to Sarabia, August 16, 1910, printed in *Artículos de Combate*, 52-53. The constitution of *Obreros Libres* is found in the same work, 33, or in Martínez Núñez, *La vida heroica*, 78.

2. For these letters see *Artículos de Combate*, 34-36, or *La vida heroica*, 79-80.

3. Martínez Núñez, *La vida heroica*, 80-85, using documents from the archives of José C. Valadés.

4. *Ibid.*, 41-42.

5. *Ibid.*, 42.

6. *Ibid.*, 45.

7. *Ibid.*, 112.

8. "Justice!" was distributed in Douglas in loose-leaf form on July 5, 1907, and reprinted in Los Angeles in *Revolución*, July 27, 1907; *Artículos de Combate*, 57-60.

9. Manuel Sarabia (using his alias "Sam"), Douglas, Arizona, to brother Tomás Sarabia (using alias "Henry Max Morton"), San Antonio, Texas, July 29, 1907, in ARE, L-E-927.

10. ARE, L-E-928. This is the first item in the Foreign Relations archives bearing Guerrero's signature.

11. Albro, *Always a Rebel*, 88-89. Lázaro Gutíerrez de Lara merits further study. A lawyer by training, he was involved in the events leading up to the Cananea strike in Sonora. Later, in Los Angeles, he was instrumental in introducing *magonistas* to leading socialists and other radicals. He became something of a national spokesman for the *revoltosos* and later followed Guerrero into battle.

12. Martínez Núñez, *La vida heroica*, 48.

13. *Ibid.*, 116.

14. Guerrero in Los Angeles to Tomás S. Labrada (the name Sarabia often used) in San Antonio, June 21, 1908, ARE, L-E-931. Guerrero told Sarabia to write him using the alias he had used often in Douglas—Jacobo Romero.

15. The Los Angeles police officers bringing the libel suits were also being paid by the Mexican government through Thomas Furlong. The purpose of the suits was to try to shut down *Revolución*, or "suppressing this miserable sheet" as Furlong wrote to Enrique Creel, Mexican ambassador to the United States. Furlong to Creel, December 20, 1907, ARE, L-E-930,

16. Martínez Núñez, *La vida heroica*, 120-121.

17. *Ibid.*, 122.

18. *Ibid.*, 48.

19. *Ibid.*, 49.

20. *Ibid.*, 127-128. The *"mátalos en caliente"* referred to an order from Díaz to shoot the rebel leaders of an 1879 revolt in Veracruz. It was during his first administration and did not become a Díaz "signature," but opponents of the regime never forgot the incident or hesitated to use it against him.

21. *Ibid.*, 129-130.

22. The evidence of this infiltration in archives of the Mexican foreign relations archive is overwhelming. See throughout ARE, L-E-918 to 954.

23. Telegram to Secretaría de Relaciones Exteriores, June 26, 1908, ARE, L-E-935.

24. Guerrero's account of the fighting at Viesca, the resulting arrests, and execution of Lugo appeared in two articles in *Regeneración* in Los Angeles in 1910. "The Death of the Heros," in the September 3 issue, and "Viesca," in the September 17 issue. Both were reprinted in several later publications. The uprising received a great deal of attention in the United States press. See, for example, *San Antonio Daily Express*, June 26, 28, 29, and July 1, 1908; *San*

Antonio Light, June 26 and 28, 1908; *St. Louis Post-Dispatch*, June 27 and 28, 1908; *Houston Chronicle*, June 28, 1908. For the American consul's reaction, see Luther T. Ellsworth to Secretary of State, Aug. 5, 1910, Justice, 90755-277.

25. Guerrero's account, "Las Vacas" appeared in *Regeneración*, September 10, 1910. U.S. reporters on the scene could see it had been a failure, whereas, Viesca, near Torreón, in the rich Laguna district of Coahuila, was far from the border and thus subject to a certain amount of "mystery." Consequently, it seemed to some Americans to be a greater indicator of impending revolution in Mexico.

26. Guerrero's "Palomas" was in *Regeneración*, September 24, 1910; *Washington Post*, July 1, 1908; Francisco R. Almada, *La Revolución en el Estado de Chihuahua*, Vol. I (Mexico: Instituto Nacional de Estudios Históricos de la Revolución Mexicana, 1964), 114-116.

27. Corral's comments were published widely in the United States. See, for example, clipping from the *San Francisco Chronicle*, June 28, 1908, in ARE, L-E-935.

4— "A Notorious Revolutionist"

1. Martínez Núñez, *La vida heroica*, 169-171. Enrique Flores Magón, not always the most reliable source, contributed notes to this chapter of *La vida heroica*.

2. Arturo M. Elías to Secretaría de Relaciones Exteriores, July 29, 1908, ARE, L-E-938.

3. Martínez Núñez, *La vida heroica*, 171-174. Martínez Núñez had access to the memoirs of Rangel in compiling this section of his study.

4. Martínez Núñez, *La vida heroica*, 51.

5. *Ibid.*, 52.

6. *Ibid.*, 53-55.

7. Antonio Lozano, Mexican consul in Los Angeles, in telegram to the Secretaría de Relaciones Exteriores, July 1908, ARE, L-E-941.

8. Furlong to M. E. Diebold, Mexican consul in St. Louis, December 18, 1908, ARE, L-E-942. Diebold was the representative of the Mexican government who had originally employed Furlong and his agency. In his two years employment, Diebold told his chiefs, Furlong had traveled 180,480 kilometers, had had as many as six agents working at one time, and had cost the Mexicans about $2,400 pesos a month. Diebold to Secretaría de Relaciones Exteriores, February 17, 1909, ARE, L-E-942.

9. A detective named Manuel Peña del Pino was hired by the Mexican vice consul in Clifton, Arizona, to try to apprehend Guerrero. In Los Angeles, the

private detective hired by Consul Lozano located Guerrero but could not locate the Los Angeles policeman, Felipe Talamantes, also in the pay of Mexico, to make the arrest. See the reports to the Secretaría de Relaciones Exteriores in ARE, L-E-942 and 943. The consuls always had to justify their unusual expenses, and some of them had to work hard to gloss over what sometimes read like B movie scripts.

10. Martínez Núñez, *La vida heroica*, 176.

11. A. V. Lomeli, Mexican consul in El Paso, to Secretaría de Relaciones Exteriores, July 26, 1909, ARE, L-E-947

12. Martínez Núñez, *La vida heroica*, 176-177

13. Luther T. Ellsworth to Assistant Secretary of State, February 22, 1910, Justice, 90755-176.

14. Guerrero to "Esteemed Friend," July 7, 1909, ARE, L-E-951.

15. *Punto Rojo*, No. 1, August 15, 1909, in ARE, L-E-947.

16. Guerrero to "Dear Friend Gustavo" in Yoakum, Texas, June 9, 1909; Guerrero to "Gustavus," July 7, 1909, written from San Antonio, in ARE, L-E-951. In these letters Guerrero was using the pseudonym "Nihil" or "Semper Nihil."

17. Martínez Núñez, *La vida heroica*, 181.

18. A. V. Lomeli, Mexican consul in El Paso, to Secretaría de Relaciones Exteriores, August 6, 1909, ARE, L-E-947.

19. Lomeli to Secretaría de Relaciones Exteriores, August 24, 1909, ARE, L-E-948.

20. Arturo M. Elías to Secretaría de Relaciones Exteriores, September 26, 1909; Elías telegram to Secretaría de Gobernación, September 28, 1909. Elías was the consul in Tucson, Arizona, but as problems in the borderlands increased, he was given special assignment to keep a watch on the *revoltosos* across the borderlands. Luther T. Ellsworth, United States consul in Ciudad Porfirio Díaz (now Piedras Negras), Coahuila, had a similar assignment for the United States Department of Justice. Both men seemed to enjoy their work. See Dorothy Pierson Kerig, *Luther T. Ellsworth: U. S. Consul on the Border During the Mexican Revolution*, Southwestern Studies No. 47 (El Paso: Texas Western Press, 1975).

21. Elías to Secretaría de Relaciones Exteriores, January 11, 1910; Elías to Secretaría de Relaciones Exteriores, February 11, 1910, ARE, L-E952. The description of Guerrero was in minute detail. Cesar Canseco, Mexican consul in Galveston to Secretaría de Relaciones Exteriores, February 17, 1910, ARE, L-E-952.

22. *Houston Chronicle*, February 14, 1910; Canseco to Secretaría de Relaciones Exteriores, February 17, 1910, ARE, L-E-952; Ellsworth to Assistant Secretary of State, February 12, 1910, Justice, 90755-175. Information on the Hotel Louisiana is from the Houston Metropolitan Research Center, Houston

Public Library. The boarding house was in existence not more than a year.

23. Martínez Núñez, *La vida heroica*, 183.

24. Ellsworth to Assistant Secretary of State, February 12, 1910, Justice 90755-175; Ellsworth to Assistant Secreaty of State, March 8, 1910, Justice, 90755-176.

25. Phrase used by United States Secretary of State Philander Knox in a letter to the Attorney General, March 28, 1910, Justice, 90755-177. Knox was simply quoting, without attribution, Ellsworth's note accompanying a manifesto he translated and sent to the Assistant Secretary of State, March 17, 1910, Justice 90755-177.

26. Martínez Núñez, *La vida heroica*, 184-185.

27. John Kenneth Turner, *Barbarous Mexico* (Chicago: Charles H. Kerr & Company, 1911), reprinted with an introduction by Sinclair Snow (Austin: University of Texas Press, 1969), 242.

28. Martínez Núñez, *La vida heroica*, 189.

29. Charles Boynton, U. S. Attorney, Western District of Texas, Waco, to Mr. J. Herbert Cole, Special Agent in Charge, San Antonio, Texas, May 21, 1910, Justice, 90755-210; Boynton to Attorney General, July 2, 1910, Justice, 90755-212.

30. Guerrero's "Program of the Pan American Labor League" was published in *Regeneración*, October 22, 1910.

31. Guerrero to Manuel Sarabia, August 16, 1910, in *Artículos de Combate*, 52-53.

32. Martínez Núñez, *La vida heroica*, 58.

33. *Regeneración*, various issues, September through December, 1910.

34. Ethel Duffy Turner, *Ricardo Flores Magón y el Partido Liberal Mexicano* (Morelia, Michoacán: Editorial "Erandi" del Gobierno del Estado, 1960), 206-207; interview with Ethel Duffy Turner in Cuernavaca, Morelos, Mexico, in June, 1965.

35. *Regeneración*, September through December, 1910.

36. Padua, *Movimiento revolucionario*, 114-121; Elena Azaola Garrido, *Rebelión y derrota de magonismo agrario* (Mexico: Fondo de Cultura Económica, 1982), 176-185.

37. Guerrero's article on Madero, entitled "He's no worker, he's bourgeois," was published in *Punto Rojo*, April 3, 1910, and reprinted in *Regeneración*, June 3, 1911.

38. E. D. Turner, *Ricardo Flores Magón*, 207; Martínez Núñez, *La vida heroica*, 223.

39. Almada, *La Revolución*, 179; Martínez Núñez, *La vida heroica*, 221-239.

40. *Regeneración*, January 14, 1911.

41. Ibid.

5—Friends And Foes

1. In 1910 the illiteracy rate in Mexico was eighty-four percent. MacLachlan and Beezley, *El Gran Pueblo*, 190-191. It could not have been much better among Mexican immigrant workers along the U.S. border, which raises questions about the audiences for the radical journalism practiced by the *PLM*. Richard Medina Estrada points out, however, that many of the *PLM* followers in the El Paso-Ciudad Juárez area were solidly middle class. See his unpublished master's thesis, "Border Revolution: the Mexican Revolution in the Ciudad Juárez-El Paso Area, 1906-1915" (El Paso: Univeristy of Texas at El Paso, 1975) 34-36. Certainly, the audience was wide enough to cause great consternation on the part of the Mexican government.

2. Raat, *Revoltosos*, 40.
3. Albro, *Always a Rebel*, 89-95.
4. Guerrero to Manuel Sarabia, May 28, 1910, in *Artículos de Combate*, 49.
5. Guerrero to Manuel Sarabia, June 16, 1910, *Ibid.*, 50.
6. Guerrero to Manuel Sarabia, August 4, 1910, *Ibid.*, 51.
7. Guerrero to Manuel Sarabia, August 16, 1910, *Ibid.*, 52-53.
8. Ricardo Flores Magón to Enrique Flores Magón, June 7, 1908, in Diego Abad de Santillán, *Ricardo Flores Magón, el apóstol de la revolución social mexicana* (Mexico: Grupo Cultural "Ricardo Flores Magón," 1925), 47-55; Ricardo Flores Magón to Enrique Flores Magón and Práxedis Guerrero, June 13 and 15, 1908, in Manuel González Ramírez, ed., *Epistolario y textos de Ricardo Flores Magón* (Mexico: Fondo de Cultura Económica, 1964), 202-209.
9. For Enrique's account of his "participation" in the attack on Palomas, see Samuel Kaplan, *"Combatimos la tiranía": Conversaciones con Enrique Flores Magón*, trans. by Jesús Amaya Topete (Mexico: Instituto Nacional de Estudios Históricos de la Revolución Mexicana, 1958), 159-170. Guerrero told Ethel Duffy Turner about Enrique's "accident" and Manuel Garza, another participant, told the same story to Nicolás T. Bernal. In research for a doctoral dissertation I interviewed Turner in Cuernavaca and Bernal in Mexico City in 1965 and both told me the same story. Piero Ferrua in his study of Guerrero (*Gli Anarchici Nella Rivoluzione Messicana*, 108) was the first to pay much attention to my charges but was not certain of the effects. James Sandos, on the other hand, thought it a most significant issue and important in driving Guerrero away from Flòres Magón. See his *Rebellion in the Borderlands: Anarchism and the Plan of San Diego, 1904-1923* (Norman: University of Oklahoma Press, 1992), 180.
10. See, for example, "Manifesto to the Workers of All Countries," dated May

10, 1909, from San Antonio, and signed by Guerrero and Enrique Flores Magón, in Justice, 90755-176, or in ARE, L-E-951.

11. The same archival records, Justice, 90755-176, and ARE, L-E-951, contain numerous copies of Guerrero's letters dealing with the issues mentioned.

12. Although incredibly detailed, the informer's report on Guerrero acquired by Mexican consul Arturo Elías in 1910 made no specific references that might shed light on Guerrero's relationships. He declared Guerrero "moderate in habits" with "no known vices." ARE, L-E-952.

13. Cockcroft, *Intellectual Precursors*, 118-119; Ward S. Albro, III, "Antonio I. Villarreal y 30 años de Revolución en México," *Anuario Veritas*, 9 (Monterrery: Universidad Regiomontana, 1990), 86. On Sara Estela Ramírez, see Inés Hernández Tovar, "Sara Estela Ramírez: The Early Twentieth Century Mexican Poet," unpublished Ph.D. dissertation (University of Houston, 1984).

14. Typical of the approach of the St. Louis press was this excerpt from an account of interviewing Andrea about the arrest of López Manzano, "Aaron Apple" to the reporter: "There was a glint in her eye which indicated she was concerned not merely because he was a fellow-countryman. Asked if the señor was her sweetheart, she laughed lightly and then cried," *St. Louis Republic*, November 20, 1906.

15. M. E. Diebold, Mexican consul in St. Louis, to Secretaría de Relaciones Exteriores, July 31, 1908, ARE, L-E-938; "Thrilling," *St. Louis Post-Dispatch*, December 16, 1906.

16. Manuel Sarabia, Douglas, Arizona, to Tomás Sarabia, San Antonio, September 19, 1907, ARE, L-E-928; letter from Tomás S. Labrada, San Antonio, to Andrea Villarreal González, St. Louis, March 16, 1908, asking for contributions to newspaper, ARE, L-E-932; *Reforma, Libertad, y Justicia*, September 25, 1908.

17. *The New York Times*, July 1, 1908.

18. See letters from Andrea Villarreal González, Phoenix, Arizona, to Mrs. Ascensión P. de Morantes, San Antonio, in 1909 in ARE, L-E-951.

19. Manuel Cuesta, Mexican consul in Del Rio, Texas, to Secretaría de Relaciones Exteriores, August 19, 1909, ARE, L-E-947; Ethel Duffy Turner, "Notes," Ethel Duffy Turner Collection, Biblioteca del Instituto Nacional de Antropología e Historia, México, D. F.

20. *La Voz de la Mujer*, supplement (October 19, 1906), No. 5 (July 28, 1907), No. 7 (August 11, 1907), No. 9 (September 6, 1907), No. 13 (October 27, 1907) in Silvestre Terrazas Collection, Bancroft Library, University of California at Berkeley; Leonor Castro [León Cárdenas], El Paso, to Antonio I. Villarreal, Los Angeles, August 11, 1907, ARE, L-E-927; *Mujer Moderna* and *El Obrero*, with excerpts and translations of articles, are discussed in Justice, 90755, and the ARE has one copy of the *El Obrero*, Vol. I, No. 8 (December 15, 1910), L-E-953. Clara Lomas has examined the issue of gender in a study for the Recovering the U.S. Hispanic Literary Heritage Project at Arte Público Press, University of Houston.

She published some of her early findings in "The Articulation of Gender in the Mexican Borderlands, 1900-1915," in Ramón Gutiérrez and Genaro Padilla, eds., *Recovering the U.S. Hispanic Literary Heritage* (Houston: Arte Público Press, 1993) 293-307.

21. Luther T. Ellsworth, U.S. consul and special U.S. border representative to the Department of Justice, received regular reports from an informant, Captain Coy, who had gained the confidence of both the Villarreal sisters. See, for example, Justice, 90755-212, 227, 229, 232.

22. "Revolutionary Women," *Artículos de Combate*, 149-150; republished in *Regeneración*, January 11, 1913.

23. "Women," *Artículos de Combate*, 137-143; *Regeneración*, November 12, 1910.

24. The *punto rojo* is found in *Artículos de Combate*, 180, and was in *Regeneración*, September 17, 1910; the program of the Pan American Labor League, drawn up in San Antonio, was printed in *Artículos de Combate*, 122-127, and in *Regeneración*, October 22, 1910.

25. Albro, *Always a Rebel*, 91-95; E.D. Turner, *Ricardo Flores Magón*, 141-145; Turner, interview, 1965; Elizabeth Darling Trowbridge, *Political Prisoners Held in the United States: Refugees Imprisoned at the Request of a Foreign Government* (Tucson: The Border Publishing Company, 1908). When Elizabeth Trowbridge and Sarabia married, the headlines proclaimed "Revolutionist Sarabia Weds Rich Boston Girl," *Tucson Citizen*, December 29, 1908; one of her uncles told the Mexican consul that she was not exactly "rich," ARE, L-E-945. Ethel Duffy Turner reported that "Elizabeth's personal fortune of more than $50,000" was used up in the cause. Ethel Duffy Turner, typescript, Ethel Duffy Turner Collection, INAH. The Sarabias returned to Mexico during the Mexican Revolution, but fled again, this time to Boston, where Manuel died of tuberculosis in 1915. His widow lived in relative poverty until she died in Brooklyn, New York, in 1934. See, E.D. Turner, *Ricardo Flores Magón*, 359-360.

26. Eugene Nolte, U.S. marshal, Western District of Texas, to Attorney General, July 3, 1909, Justice, 90755-121. It probably never occurred to Nolte that the fact he could not understand the language might have contributed to the way he characterized Mexicans. In the same report he mentioned that his deputy on the border did not speak Spanish but had wide experience and "unlimited support of every officer in Eagle Pass, which is a more valuable asset to him than the mere ability to speak the language." Ellsworth's comments about Mexican character are found throughout Justice files.

27. *St. Louis Post-Dispatch*, November 20, 1906.

28. *The New York Times*, July 1, 1908.

29. The report "Some of the cases in which Mexican Refugees in the United States of America have been victims of Persecutions an Kidnappings" was translated into English by Ellsworth, Justice, 90755-176.

30. R. Flores Magón to E. Flores Magón, June 7, 1908.

31. "Something Else," *Artículos de Combate*, 92-94; *Regeneración*, September 3, 1910.

32. "Whites, Whites," *Artículos de Combate*, 144-145; *Regeneración*, November 19, 1910. Rodríguez had been accused of killing a white woman on a ranch near Rocksprings, Texas. See, Arnold de León, *Mexican Americans in Texas: A Brief History* (Arlington Heights, Illinois: Harlan Davidson, Inc., 1993), 50.

6—*"Gli Anarchici Nella Rivoluzione Messicana"*

1. The title of this chapter, taken from Piero Ferrua's study of Guerrero, *The Anarchists in the Mexican Revolution*, is a reflection of how the Mexicans probably received more attention, recognition, and appreciation for their commitment to anarchism from Europe than from North America.

2. This discussion of the development of anarchism is based generally on the following: Paul Avrich, *The Russian Anarchists* (Princeton: Princeton University Press, 1967); Avrich, *An American Anarchist: The Life Of Voltairine de Cleyre* (Princeton: Princeton University Press, 1978); Avrich, *Anarchist Portraits* (Princeton: Princeton University Press, 1988); John M. Hart, *Anarchism and the Mexican Working Class, 1860-1931* (Austin: University of Texas Press, 1978); James Joll, *The Anarchists* (New York: Grosset and Dunlap, 1966); Alan Ritter, *Anarchism: A Theoretical Analysis* (Cambridge: Cambridge University Press, 1980); and George Woodcock, *Anarchism: A History of Libertarian Ideas and Movements* (Cleveland: The World Company, 1962). The quote is from Woodcock, *Anarchism*, 425.

3. Joll, *The Anarchists*, 150.

4. This discussion has not gone into anarcho-syndicalism, which became more significant to the anarchist movement after Guerrero's death, and influenced some of the later ideas of Flores Magón. The anarcho-syndicalists represented the ideas of industrial workers, waging total war with the capitalist system. These ideas came to dominate groups such as the Industrial Workers of the World, who had numerous contacts with the *magonistas*, especially after 1910. Guerrero did seem to be very much influenced by Tarrida de Mármol, Malatesta, and others who argued for "anarchy without adjectives." Eliminate the state, and then worry about resolving differences about what comes after. See Avrich, *An American Anarchist*, 149-157.

5. Hart, *Anarchism*, particularly 3-18.

6. John Mason Hart, typescript of "The Evolution of Mexican and Mexican-American Working Class Values," the introduction to John Mason Hart, *Meeting the Challenges: Mexican and Mexican-American Workers in Transition* (Wilmington, Delaware: Scholarly Resources, 1996).

7. A provocative discussion of these influences is found in Shawn L. England, "Anarquismo or Indigenismo? The Rural Origins of Ricardo Flores Magón's Libertarian-Socialist Political Philosophy," paper presented at the annual meeting of the Rocky Mountain Council for Latin American Studies, Vancouver, British Columbia, Canada, April 1993.

8. Albro, *Always a Rebel*, 28-29, 25; Cockcroft, *Intellectual Precursors*, 118-119.

9. Albro, *Always a Rebel*, 101-104, 140-142. My ideas on Flores Magón's anarchism are by no means the only interpretation. Other views, generally seeing him a committed anarchist much earlier, are found in Cockcroft, *Intellectual Precursors*; Hernández Padilla, *El Magonismo*; Juan Gómez-Quiñones, *Sembradores: Ricardo Flores Magón y el Partido Liberal Mexicano: A Eulogy and Critique* (Los Angeles: University of California Press, 1973); among others.

10. This was part of the description of Guerrero Mexican Consul Arturo Elías obtained in 1910 from an informer who knew Práxedis in Arizona in 1906 and 1907, ARE, L-E-952.

11. Martínez Núñez, *La vida heroica*, 48.

12. *Ibid.* 129.

13. Ricardo Flores Magón to Enrique Flores Magón and Práxedis Guerrero, June 13 and 15, 1908.

14. Martínez Núñez, *La vida heroica*, 176.

15. *Ibid.*, 56.

16. *Regeneración*, September 17, 1910.

17. *Ibid*, September 10, 1910.

18. *Ibid.*, November 5, 1910.

19. *Ibid.*, October 8, 1910.

7— "Writing, Writing, Writing"

1. Nicolás Chavira, *Informe rendido con motivo de la traslación de los restos del Gral. Práxedis G. Guerrero* (Chihuahua: Talleres Gráficas del Gobierno Chihuahua, 1935).

2. As mentioned earlier, copies of *Regeneración* are available in several depositories, but copies of *Punto Rojo* and *Revolución* are hard to find. The archive at the Ministry of Foreign Relations in Mexico has some copies of *Punto Rojo* and Martínez Núñez had access to a few others. *Revolución* was collected rather effectively by Foreign Relations.

3. Práxedis G. Guerrero, *Artículos Literarios y de Combate; Pensamientos; Crónicas Revolucionarias, etc.* (Mexico: Grupo Cultural "Ricardo Flores Magón," 1924).

4. *Regeneración, 1900-1918, La corriente más radical de la revolución mexicana de 1910 a través de su periódo de combate*,Prólogo, selección y notas de Armando Bartra (Mexico: Ediciones Era, 1977 and many other editions).

5. *Práxedis G.Guerrero, Artículos de Combate* (Mexico: Ediciones Antorcha, 1984); *Vocación de Libertad, Práxedis J.* [sic] *Guerrero*; prólogo: José Muñoz Cota; presentación, Celso H. Delgado (Guanajuato: Ediciones del Estado de Guanajuato, 1977). Cortés, a native of León, resides in Mexico City, but retains interests in León, including a bookstore named, appropriately, "El Ahuizote."

6. Cockcroft, *Intellectual Precursors*, 68.

7. Ralph Chaplin, *Wobbly, the Rough-and-Tumble Story of an American Radical* (Chicago: University of Chicago Press, 1948), 117, 310.

8. Ricardo Flores Magón, Federal Penitentiary, Leavenworth, Kansas, to Nicolás T. Bernal, Mexico, D. F., July 23, 1922, in *Práxedis G. Guerrero, Artículos Literarios*, 11.

9. In this discussion of Guerrero's writings, the citations will refer to the location of the article in each of the folowing, where applicable: the 1924 collection will be cited as *Guerrero*; the collection entitled *Regeneración* edited by Armando Bartra will cited as *Bartra* to avoid confusion with the newspaper; the collection of Ediciones Antorcha will be cited as *Artículos*; finally there will be citation of where and when first published, if known. The citation for Justice! is *Artículos*, 57-60; *Revolución*, July 27, 1907.

10. *Guerrero*, 83-84; *Bartra*, 187-188; *Artículos*, 61-62; *Revolución*, September 14, 1907.

11. *Artículos*, 63-64; *Revolución*, November 9, 1907.

12. *Guerrero*, 24; *Artículos*, 65; *Revolución*, November 9, 1907.

13. *Guerrero*, 51-52; *Artículos*, 66-67; *Revolución*, December 14, 1907.

14. *Guerrero*, 85-86; *Artículos*, 68-69; *Revolución*, January 25, 1908.

15. Although many articles from *Punto Rojo* have been published, and several were republished in *Regeneración*, the only copies of the newspaper I have seen were in the Foreign Relations archives in Mexico City (ARE).

16. *Artículos*, 76-77; *Punto Rojo*, August 29, 1909.

17. *Ibid.*

18. *Ibid.*

19. *Ibid.*

20. *Artículos*, 85-86; *Punto Rojo*, September 26, 1909.

21. Martínez Núñez, *La vida heroica*, 56.

22. *Guerrero* (edited version), 90-91; *Artículos*, 92-94; *Regeneración*, September 3, 1910.

23. *Guerrero*, 74-76; *Bartra*, 193-194; *Artículos*, 95-97; *Regeneración*, September 10, 1910.

24. *Guerrero*, 53-55; *Bartra*, 191-193; *Artículos*, 98-100; *Regeneración*, September 17, 1910.

25. *Guerrero*, 25-27; *Artículos*, 101-102; *Regeneración*, September 17, 1910.

26. *Guerrero*, 28; *Artículos*, 103; *Regeneración*, September 17, 1910.

27. *Guerrero*, 77-79; *Bartra*, 204-205; *Artículos*, 104-106; *Regeneración*, September 24, 1910.

28. *Guerrero*, 46-48; *Bartra*, 220-221; *Artículos*, 168-170; *Regeneración*, September 3, 1910. This is included in all the collections with acccounts of the three conflicts which follow, under the title, "Revolutionary Episodes."

29. "Las Vacas" in *Guerrero*, 29-36; *Bartra*, 211-215; *Artículos*, 153-159; *Regeneración*, September 10, 1910. "Viesca" in *Guerrero*, 36-42; *Bartra*, 215-218; *Artículos*, 160-163; *Regeneración*, September 17, 1910. "Palomas" in *Guerrero*, 42-46; *Bartra*, 218- 220; *Artículos*, 164-167; *Regeneración*, September 24, 1910.

30. *Guerrero*, 87-89; *Bartra*, 222-223; *Artículos*, 108-110; *Regeneración*, October 1, 1910.

31. Paul Avrich, *The Modern School Movement: Anarchism and Education in the United States* (Princeton: Princeton University Press, 1980), 3-33; Joll, *The Anarchists*, 232-237; Woodcock, *Anarchism*, 370-372.

32. *Guerrero*, 80-82; *Artículos*, 111-113; *Regeneración*, October 1, 1910.

33. *Guerrero*, 58-62; *Bartra*, 207-209; *Artículos*, 114-117; *Regeneración*, October 8, 1910.

34. *Artículos*, 128-131; *Regeneración*, October 29, 1910.

35. *Guerrero*, 70-73; *Bartra*, 196-198; *Artículos*, 118-121; *Regeneración*, October 8, 1910.

36. *Guerrero*, 56-57; *Bartra*, 195-196; *Artículos*, 132-133; *Regeneración*, November 5, 1910.

37. *Guerrero*, 63-69; *Bartra*, 199-203; *Artículos*, 137-143; *Regeneración*, November 12, 1910.

38. *Guerrero*, 95-96; *Bartra*, 251-252; *Artículos*, 144-145; *Regeneración*, November 19, 1910.

39. "Revolutionary Women" in *Guerrero*, 49-50; *Bartra*, 198-199; *Artículos*, 149-150; but it was not reprinted in *Regeneración* until January 11, 1913. A sample of the "Victoria Segura" work is "White Ideal on a Red Standard," published in *El Obrero*, August 1910 and reprinted in *Regeneración*, February 18, 1911. See translation by Luther Ellsworth in Justice, 90755-227, and Spanish version in *Artículos*, 147.

40. The "red dots" are found in *Guerrero*, 97-108; a selected collection in

Bartra, 209-211; and the actual newspaper excerpts from *Regeneración* from September to November 1910 in *Artículos de Combate*, 173-203.

41. *Guerrero*, 16-17; *Artículos de Combate*, 12; *Regeneración*, January 14, 1911.

8 — Poet-Revolutionary

1. See Juan Gómez-Quiñones, *Roots of Chicano Politics, 1600-1940* (Albuquerque: University of New Mexico Press, 1994) and Gómez-Quiñones, *Mexican American Labor, 1790-1990* (Albuquerque: University of New Mexico Press, 1994); Emilio Zamora, *The World of the Mexican Worker in Texas* (College Station: Texas A&M University Press, 1993).

BIBLIOGRAPHY

Archives and Archival Collections

Magonismo, Legajos 918 to 954, Archivo "Genaro Estrada" de Secretaría de Relaciones Exteriorers, Mexico, D. F.
United States Department of Justice, Record Group 74, Files 90755 and 180187, National Archives, Washington, D. C.
Ethel Duffy Turner Collection, Biblioteca del Instituto Nacional de Antropología e Historia, Mexico, D. F.
Silvestre Terrazas Collection, Bancroft Library, University of California, Berkeley, California.
Revoltosos, 1906 y 1908, Archivo General de la Nación, Mexico, D. F.
Archivo Histórico Municipal de León, Guanajuato
Office of Archives, Federal Bureau of the Prisons, United States Department of Justice, Washington, D. C.

Publications of Grupo Cultural "Ricardo Flores Magón" in Mexico, D. F.

Abad de Santillán, Diego. *Ricardo Flores Magón, el apóstol de la revolución social mexicana*. 1925.
Flores Magón, Ricardo. *Epistolario revolucionario e íntimo* 3 vols. 1925.
_____. *Sembrando Ideas*. 1923.
_____. *Semilla Libertaria*. 2 vols. 1923.
_____. *Tribuna Roja*. 1925.
_____. *Tierra y Libertad*. 1924.
_____. *Verdugos y Víctimas*. 1924.
Práxedis G. Guerrero, *Artículos literarios y de combate; pensamientos; crónicas revolucionarios, etc.* 1924.
(The next two items were published before the *Grupo Cultural* was formally organized with support for the publication program from the Mexican government.)
Vida nueva. Comité de agitación por la libertad de Ricardo Flores Magón y compañeros presos en Estados Unidos del Norte. n.d.
Por la libertad de Ricardo Flores Magón y compañeros presos en Estados Unidos del Norte. 1922.

*Publications of Ediciones Antorcha in Mexico, D. F.
Compiled and edited by Chantal López and Omar Cortés*

Abad de Santillán, Diego. *Ricardo Flores Magón, el apóstol de la revolución mexicana.* 1988.
Beas, Juan Carlos and Manuel Ballesteros, *Movimiento indígena y magonismo en México.* 1987.
Flores Magón, Enrique. *Frente al enemigo.* 1987.
_____. *En pos de la libertad.* 1988.
Flores Magón, Ricardo. *Epistolario e íntimo.* 1983.
_____. *¿Para qué sirve la autoridad? y otros cuentos.* 1981.
_____. *En defensa de la revolución.* 1988.
_____. *Artículos políticos, 1910.* 1980.
_____. *Artículos políticos, 1911.* 1980.
_____. *Artículos políticos, 1912.* 1981.
_____. *El miedo del gobierno (Artículos políticos, 1912).* 1981.
_____. *Artículos políticos, 1914.* 1982.
_____. *1914: La intervención americana en México.* 1981.
_____. *Carranza contra los trabajadores (Artículos políticos, 1915).* 1987.
_____. *La primera guerra mundial y la revolución rusa.* 1983.
_____. *Obras de teatro. Tierra y Libertad. Verdugos y víctimas.* 1987.
Práxedis G. Guerrero. Artículos de Combate. 1986.
El Partido Liberal Mexicano (1906-1908). 1986.
El Programa del Partido Liberal Mexicano de 1906 y sus antecedentes. 1985.
Rivera, Librado. *¡Viva Tierra y Libertad!* 1980.

Books and Articles

Albro, Ward S. *Always a Rebel: Ricardo Flores Magón and the Mexican Revolution.* Fort Worth: Texas Christian University Press, 1992.
_____. "Antonio I. Villarreal y 30 años de revolución en Mexico," *Anuario Veritas,* 9. Monterrey: Universidad Regiomontana, 1990, 82-115.
_____. "El secuestro de Manuel Sarabia," *Historia Mexicana,* 18, (Jan.-March 1969), 400-407.
Almada, Francisco R. *La Revolución en el Estado de Chihuahua.* Mexico: Instituto Nacional de Estudios Históricos de la Revolución Mexicana, 1964.
Avrich, Paul. *An American Anarchist: The Life of Voltairine de Cleyre.* Princeton: Princeton University Press, 1978.
_____. *Anarchist Portraits.* Princeton: Princeton University Press, 1988.
_____. *The Modern School Movement: Anarchism and Education in the*

United States. Princeton: Princeton University Press, 1980.
_____. *The Russian Anarchists*. Princeton: Princeton University Press, 1967.
Azaola, Elena. *Rebelión y derrota de magonismo agrario*. Mexico: Fondo de Cultura Económica, 1982.
Barreiro Tablada, Enrique. *Práxedis Guerrero, un fragmento de la revolución*. Córdoba, Veracruz: Ediciones Norte, 1928.
The Border (Tucson, Arizona).
Chaplin, Ralph. *Wobbly, the Rough-and-Tumble Story of an American Radical*. Chicago: University of Chicago Press, 1948.
Chavira, Nicolás. *Informe rendido con motivo de la traslación de los restos del Gral. Práxedis G. Guerrero*. Chihuahua: Talleres Gráficas del Gobierno Chihuahua, 1935.
Cockcroft, James. *Intellectual Precursors of the Mexican Revolution, 1900-1913*. Austin: University of Texas Press, 1968.
Cosío Villegas, Daniel. *Historia moderna de México*. 7 vols. Mexico: Editorial Hermes, 1965-1975.
De Leon, Arnoldo. *Mexican Americans in Texas: A Brief History*.Arlington Heights, Illinois: Harlan Davidson, Inc., 1993.
England, Shawn L. "Anarquismo or Indigenismo? The Rural Origins of Ricardo Flores Magón's Libertarian-Socialist Political Philosophy. Paper presented at the Annual Meeting of the Rocky Mountain Council for Latin American Studies, Vancouver, British Columbia, Canada, April 1993.
Estrada, Richard Medina. "Border Revolution: The Mexican Revolution in the Ciudad Juárez-El Paso Area, 1906-1915. Unpublished Master's Thesis, University of Texas at El Paso, 1975.
Fabela, Isidro. *fundador. Documentos históricos de la Revolución Mexicana*, X, *Actividades políticas y revolucionarias de los hermanos Flores Magón*. Mexico: Editorial Jus, S.A., 1966.
_____. *Documentos históricos de la Revolución Mexicana*, XI, *Precursors de la Revolución Mexicana, 1906-1910*. Mexico: Editorial Jus, S.A., 1966.
Ferrua, Piero. *Gli Anarchici Nella Rivoluzione Messicana: Práxedis G. Guerrero*. Ragusa: Edizione "La Fiasccola," 1976.
Flores Magón, Ricardo. *La Revolución Mexicana*. Mexico: Editores Mexicanos Unidos, S. A., 1985.
Furlong, Thomas. *Fifty Years a Detective*. St. Louis: C. E. Barnett, 1912.
Gómez-Quiñones, Juan. *Sembradores: Ricardo Flores Magón y el Partido Liberal Mexicano: A Eulogy and Critique*. Los Angeles: University of California Press, 1973.
_____. *Mexican American Labor, 1790-1990*. Albuquerque: University of New Mexico Press, 1994.

_____. *Roots of Chicano Politics, 1600-1940.* Albuquerque: University of New Mexico Press, 1994.
González Ramírez, Manuel, ed. *Epistolario y textos de Ricardo Flores Magón.* Mexico: Fondo de Cultura Económica, 1964.
Hart, John Mason. *Anarchism and the Mexican Working Class, 1860-1931.* Austin: University of Texas Press, 1978.
_____. *The Coming and Process of the Mexican Revolution.* Berkeley: University of California Press, 1987.
_____, ed. *Meeting the Challenges: Mexican and Mexican-Workers in Transition.* Wilmington, Delaware: Scholarly Resources, 1996.
Los Hermanos Flores Magón: Manifesto del Partido Liberal Mexicano. Mexico: Instituto Nacional de Estudios Históricos de la Revolución Mexicana, 1985.
Hernández Padilla, Salvador. *El Magonismo: Historia de una pasión libertaria, 1900-1922.* Mexico: Ediciones Era, 1984.
Hernández Tovar, Inés. "Sara Estela Ramírez: the Early Twentieth Century Mexican Poet." Unpublished Ph.D. dissertation, University of Houston, 1984.
Ibarra Grande, Pbro. Jesùs. *Jaral de Berrio y su Marquesada.* León, Guanajuato, 1990.
Joll, James. *The Anarchists.* New York: Grosset and Dunlapp, 1966.
Kaplan, Samuel. *"Combatimos la tiranía:" Conversaciones con Enrique Flores Magón.* Translated by Jesús Amaya Topete. Mexico: Instituto Nacional de Estudios Históricos de la Revolución Mexicana, 1958.
Katz, Friedrich. "The Liberal Republic and the Porfiriato" in Leslie Bethell, ed. *Mexico Since Independence.* Cambridge: Cambridge University Press, 1991.
Kerig, Dorothy Pierson. *Luther T. Ellsworth: U. S. Consul on the Border during the Mexican Revolution.* Southwestern Studies No. 47. El Paso: Texas Western Press, 1975.
Lomas, Clara. "The Articulation of Gender in the Mexico Borderlands, 1900-1915." In Ramón Gutiérrez and Genaro Padilla, eds. *Recovering the U.S. Hispanic Literary Heritage.* Houston: Arte Público Press, 1993.
MacLachlan, Colin. *Anarchism and the Mexican Revolution: The Political Trials of Ricardo Flores Magón in the United States.* Berkeley: University of California Press, 1991.
_____ and William H. Beezley. *El Gran Pueblo: A History of Greater Mexico.* Englewood Clliffs, N. J.: Prentice Hall, 1994.
Martínez Núñez, Eugenio. *La vida heroica de Práxedis G. Guerrero.* Mexico: Instituto Nacional de Estudios Históricos de la Revolución, 1960.
Meyer, Michael C, and William L. Sherman. *The Course of Mexican History.*

5th ed. New York: Oxford University Press, 1995.
Navarro Valtierra, Carlos Arturo. "El periodo revolucionario en la historia de León," *Tiempos*, (Nov.-Dec. 1993) Archivo Histórico Municipal de León, Guanajuato, 3-8.
Nexos, 68, September 1993.
Padua, Cándido Donato. *Movimiento revolucionario 1906 en Veracruz*, 2nd ed. Tlalpán, D. F.: n.p. 1941.
Poole, David, ed. *Land and Liberty: Anarchist Influences in the Mexican Revolution: Ricardo Flores Magón*. Sanday, Orkney, U.K.: Cienfuegos Press, 1977.
Raat, W. Dirk. *Revoltosos: Mexico's Rebels in the United States, 1903-1923*. College Station: Texas A&M University Press, 1981.
Regeneración, 1900-1918. La corriente más radical de la revolución mexicana de 1910 a través de su periodo de combate. Prólogo, selección y notas de Armando Bartra. Mexico: Ediciones Era, 1977.
Ritter, Alan. *Anarchism: A Theoretical Analysis*. Cambridge: Cambridge University Press, 1980.
Sandos, James. *Rebellion in the Borderlands: Anarchism and the Plan of San Diego, 1904-1923*. Norman: University of Oklahoma Press, 1992.
Sarabia, Manuel. "How I Was Kidnapped," *The Border* (Tucson, Arizona) Vol. I, No. 2 (Dec. 1908), 1-4.
Trowbridge, Elizabeth Darling. *Political Prisoners Held in the United States: Refugees Imprisoned at the Request of a Foreign Government*. Tucson: The Border Publishing Comapny, 1908.
Turner, Ethel Duffy. *Ricardo Flores Magón y el Partido Liberal Mexicano*. Morelia, Michoacán: Editorial "Erandi" del Gobierno del Estado, 1960.
Turner, John Kenneth. *Barbarous Mexico*. Chicago: Charles H. Kerr & Company, 1911. Reprinted with an introduction by Sinclair Snow, Austin: University of Texas Press, 1969.
Vanderwood, Paul J. *Disorder and Progress: Bandits, Police, and Mexican Development*. 2nd ed. rev. Wilmington, Delaware: Scholarly Resources, Inc., 1992.
Vocación de Libertad: Práxedis J. [sic] Guerrero. Prólogo: José Muñoz Cota; presentación: Celso H. Delgado. Guanajuato: Ediciones del Estado de Guanajuato, 1977.
Woodcock, George. *Anarchism: A History of Liberation Ideas and Movements*. Cleveland: Meridien Books, The World Company, 1962.
Zamora, Emilio. *The World of the Mexican Worker in Texas*. College Station: Texas A&M University Press, 1993.

Newspapers

The Arizona Daily Star (Tucson)
El Paso Herald
Houston Chronicle
International American (Douglas, Arizona)
Mujer Moderna (San Antonio)
New York Times
El Obrero (San Antonio)
Punto Rojo (El Paso)
Reforma, Libertad, y Justicia (Austin, Texas, and McAlester, Indian Territory)
Regeneración (San Antonio, St. Louis, and Los Angeles)
Revolución (Los Angeles)
St. Louis Post-Dispatch
St. Louis Republic
San Antonio Daily Express
San Antonio Light
San Francisco Call
San Francisco Chronicle
Tucson Citizen
La Voz de la Mujer (El Paso)
Washington Post

Interviews

Nicolás T. Bernal, Mexico City, June 1965.
Francisco Longoria, Los Altos de Ibarra, Guanajuato, April 1994.
Carlos Arturo Navarro Valtierra, León, Guanajuato, April 1994.
Ethel Duffy Turner, Cuernavaca, Morelos, June 1965.

INDEX

Acayucán, Veracruz, 25
Agis, S. T., 57
Aguilar, José R., 38
Aguirre, Lauro, 24, 26, 55, 75, 82
Alba Roja (San Francisco), 14, 72, 103, 116
Albertos, _____, 127
Albuquerque, New Mexico, 48, 77
Altos de Ibarra, Los (Guanajuato), 7, 9-12, 49, 50
American Can Company (San Francisco), 48
American consular agent, 41
American Federation of Labor, 89
American press, 89
American Southwest, 71, 114, 138. See also U.S.-Mexico borderlands.
anarchism, 76, 93, 101 139, 140; development of anarchist thought, 94-100; anarchism in Mexico, 100-104; anarchism Ricardo Flores Magón, 104-108; anarchism of Guerrero, 108-112
anarcho-communism, 99
"Anniversary," 120, 141
Anzalde, Eugenio, 38
Appeal to Reason, The, 52
Araujo, Antonio de P., 23, 41-42, 45, 78, 81
"Argument of Filogonio, The," 131-132, 149-153
Arizméndez, Federico, 35, 37
Arizona (Territory of), 20, 23, 39, 41, 47-50, 52-53, 60, 73, 81, 84, 87, 89, 122
Arizona Rangers, 20, 23, 27
Arredondo, Juan José, 24, 25

Arriaga, Camilo, 16-19, 23, 101
Austin, Texas, 42
Austria, 97

Bakunin, Mikhail, 11, 32, 94, 96-104
Barbarous Mexico, 50, 59, 84
Barcelona, Spain, 129-130
Bartra, Armando, 115, 134
Battle of Puebla (May 5, 1862), 2, 11
Bazora, Francisco, 101
"Beggar," 119
Bernal, Nicolás T., 114
"Blow," 124
Border, The (Tucson), 84
Boston, Massachusetts, 84
"Boxer, The," 118, 135
Boynton (U. S. Attorney), 52
Bridgeport, Texas 58-60, 74
Brousse Talavera, María, 84
bullfights, 9
Bustamante, Rosalío, 19

Cabrera, Luis, 139
cajas de communidad, 100
California (state), 47, 61, 64, 73, 77, 79, 84, 104, 136, 138
Canada, 19, 30, 34
Cananea, Sonora, 20, 25, 30
Cananea Consolidated Copper Company, 20
Cano, José, 26
capitalism, 96; foreign, 54
Cárdenas, Isidra T. de, 82
Cárdenas, León, 33, 59, 82
Carranza, Venustiano, 139
Casas Grandes, Chihuahua, 42, 65, 66

Catholic Church and Catholicism, 5, 8, 9
Census of 1910 (Mexican), 6
Cervantes, Miguel de, 8
Cervecería Cuauhtémoc (Monterrey), 5
Cervecería de San Luis (San Luis Potosí), 9
Chaplin, Ralph, 115
Chicago, Illinois, 72, 85
Chihuahua (City), 113
Chihuahua (state), 6, 27, 38-39, 47, 50, 64, 113
Ciudad Guzmán, Chihuahua, 48, 65
Ciudad Juárez, Chihuahua, 26, 40, 44, 50, 65
Ciudad Juárez Police Department, 57, 87, 88
Clifton, Arizona, 31, 72
Coahuila (state), 24-25, 27
Cockcroft, James, 115
Cole, J. Herbert, 57
Colmillo Público, El (Mexico City), 19-21
Colorado (state), 13
Colorado Supply Company, The (Denver), 13
Columbus, New Mexico, 44
Communism, 97
Comtean Positivism, 3
Conquest of Bread, The, 99
Constitution of 1857, 4, 7, 16
Constitution of 1917, 21
Copper mines (Arizona), 14
Corral, Román, 45
Corralitos, Chihuahua, 65
Corregidora, La (Laredo), 79
Correo Mexicano, El (Los Angeles), 36-37
Creel, Enrique, 26, 28, 64
Cortés, Omar, 115

Darwin, Charles, 8, 98-99, 102
Debs, Eugene V., 52
Defensor del Pueblo, El (Tucson), 84-85
Del Rio, Texas, 23-24, 41
Demófilo, El (San Luis Potosí), 17
Derby, Texas, 60
Despertador, El (San Felipe, Guanajuato), 8
Detectives, private, 29, 87-88, 102
Detroit Copper Mining Company Smelter (Morenci, Arizona), 14
Diario del Hogar, El (Mexico City), 10, 17, 116
Díaz government, 38, 53, 65, 108. See also Díaz, Porfirio, and Porfiriato.
Díaz, Modesto, 35-37
Díaz, Porfirio, 20. 23, 37, 54-55, 64, 67, 71, 81, 89, 93; establishment of power, 1-5; development of opposition to, 14-16; Guerrero's attacks on, 116, 118, 120, 128, 131, 132, 143
Díaz Guerra, Emcarnación, 42, 49, 127
Díaz Mirón, 8
Díaz Soto y Gama, Antonio, 16-17, 101, 139
Douglas, Arizona, 23, 27, 31-34, 48, 73, 76-77, 116
Dolson, Ethel Mowbray, 84
Durango (state), 64

Ediciones Antorcha, 115, 134
El Paso, Texas, 13, 23-26, 33, 38, 40, 42, 48-49, 53-55, 65, 77-78, 87-88, 104, 119-122, 136
Elías, Arturo M., 55, 57
Ellsworth, Luther, 85
England, 73, 95, 98-99
Enquiry Concerning Political Justice, 95
Escuela Moderna, 129-131

Espinosa, Cristóbal, 31-32
Espinoza, Tomás, 23
Evolución Social (Toyah, Texas), 59

feminism, 83, 156-163
Ferrer y Guardia, Francisco, 32, 94, 104, 129-131
Figueroa, Anselmo L., 61
First International Workingmen's Association, 96-97
Flammarión, Camille, 8
Flores Magón brothers, 17, 39, 76-77
Flores Magón, Enrique, 34, 52, 54-55, 60-62, 104-105; in origins of opposition, 16-18; relations with Guerrero, 35, 37, 39-40, 42, 45, 48-49, 76-78
Flores Magón, Jesús, 16, 17
Flores Magón, Ricardo, 14, 21, 23-24, 30-34, 36-37, 40, 49-50, 52, 54, 60-62, 64, 73, 75, 77-78, 81, 84, 114-117, 122; attitude toward *norteamericanos*, 88-89; development of Flores Magón movement, 15-19; flight and capture, 26-28; meeting with Guerrero, 35, 76; on anarchism, 93-94, 98-102, 104-108, 112; on death of Guerrero, 66, 136; significance in Mexican history, 138-140
Foreign Relations Office (Mexico), 55
France, 96, 98; French intervention, 2; French Revolution, 52, 94, 95, 102; intellectuals, 96; *philosophes*, 102
Fundiciones, Las, 9, 49
Fundidora de Fierro y Acero (Monterrey), 5
Furlong, Thomas, 28, 52
Furlong Detective Agency, 20, 26, 52

Galveston, Texas, 57
García, Clemente, 57
Germany, 97

González, Manuel, 1, 3
Godwin, William, 94-96
Goldman, Emma, 101
Gómez-Quiñones, Juan, 139
Gorky, Maksim, 11
Greene, William C., 20, 25
"Grito de Dolores," 127
Grupo Cultural "Ricardo Flores Magón," 114-115
Guanajuato (state), 2, 7, 9, 30-31, 49, 72, 78, 103
Guerrero, José de la Luz, 7, 11, 37
Guerrero, Fructuosa Hurtado de, 7, 13, 34, 78
Guerrero, Práxedis G., 2, 11-12, 15, 17-19, 21, 24, 27-28, 34, 38, 41-42, 47-50, 60-62, 64-65, 71, 78, 84, 137, 141-143, 145, 147, 149, 153, 156, 163; affiliation with *PLM*, 29-33; attack on Janos, 65-67; attack on Palomas, 42, 44-45; as writer, 33, 108-136, 141-167; departure from Mexico to U.S., 13-14; escape from capture, 47-48, 57-59; experience in Second Military Reserve, 10, 78; family of, 31, 38, 49-50; on anarchism, 93-94, 98-99, 102-105; on discrimination against Mexicans in the U.S., 85, 87-91; on feminism, 82-83, 156-63; *Punto Rojo*, 55-57; relations with Enrique Flores Magón, 39-40, 76-77; relations with Ricardo Flores Magón, 35-37, 76-77; relations with Manuel Sarabia, 72-76; relations with Villarreal González sisters, 79, 81-82; significance of, 138-140; sisters of, 37, 55, 57, 59, 61, 64, 78, 108, 122; travels in U.S., 52-54
Gutiérrez de Lara, Lázaro, 34, 50, 61, 65, 78
Guzmán, Martín Luis, 139

hacendado-peón, 137
Hacienda Los Hornos, 41
Haldeman, Julius, 52
Hart, John Mason, 100-101
Heraldo de Comercio, El (León, Guanajuato), 8
Hermosillo, Sonora, 33
Hernández, Francisco, 8
Hernández, Pedro, 8
Hidalgo, Father Miguel, 120
Hijo del Ahuizote, El (also *El Padre, El Nieto, El Bisnieto*, all in Mexico City), 17-18
Hotel Louisiana (Houston, Texas), 57
Houston, Texas, 57-58
Houston Chronicle, 57
Hugo, Victor, 8
"Hungryopolis," 54, 87

"I Am Action," 124, 126
Ibarra, Benito, 41
Illinois (state), 52
Indian Territory (Oklahoma), 48-49
"Inconvenience of Gratitude, The," 126
Industrial Workers of the World, 115
Italian anarchists, 107
Italy, 97
"International League of Workers," 60
Irontown, Missouri, 25

Janos, Chihuahua, 66, 91, 109, 136, 140
jefe político (Casas Grandes, Chihuahua), 65
Jiménez, Coahuila, 24
Juárez, Benito, 2, 3, 16
Junta Organizadora del Partido Liberal Mexicano, 18, 21, 30, 32-33, 35, 76, 82, 85
"Justice," 116

Kankum, 127

Kansas (state), 52
Kosterlitski, Emilio, 20, 27
Kropotkin, Pyotr, 11, 32, 94, 98-99, 101-104, 112

Lamartine, 8
Lampazos, Nuevo León, 17-18, 79
Lancaster, Fred, 53, 57-58
Laredo, Texas, 10, 18, 79
Las Vacas, Coahuila, 41-42, 48-49, 54, 62, 65, 81, 104, 127
"Las Vacas," 127
Leavenworth Penitentiary, 49, 114-115
Leavenworth, Kansas, 88, 114
León, Guanajuato, 7, 13, 9-10, 49-50, 102, 115-116
Lerdo de Tejado, Sebastián, 3
"Let's Push Rational Education," 131
"Let's Work, Fighters," 117
Liberals or Liberal Party. See *Partido Liberal Mexicano*.
Lira, José, 8
"Listen," 118, 141
López, Chantal, 115
López Manzano, Aaron, 25, 79
Los Angeles, California, 26, 28, 32-35, 38-39, 49, 52, 66, 73, 75-77, 84, 89, 104, 115-116, 122
Los Angeles County Jail and Police, 28, 35-36, 40, 76, 52, 84, 89, 104
Lowe, William, 54, 57
Lugo, José, 41, 61, 127

Madero, Francisco I., 6, 11, 18-19, 62, 64-65, 128, 139
Madrid, Otilo (Francisco Manrique), 44
magonistas, 20-21, 23, 40, 48, 52, 61-62, 65, 78-79, 82, 84, 87, 101-102, 112, 120, 128, 134, 138. See also *Partido Liberal Mexicano*.

"Make Way," 116, 142-143
Malatesta, Errico, 32, 99-100, 104
Manrique, Francisco, 9, 13, 30-31, 38-39, 44, 47, 49, 72, 74, 76- 77, 113
Martínez Núñez, Eugenio, 32, 35
Marx, Karl, and Marxism, 81, 96-98, 100-101
Mata, Filomeno, 10
"mátalos en caliente," 38
Matamoros, Coahuila, 41
Maximilian and Carlota, 2
"The Means and the End," 110, 133, 147-149
Mexican Americans, 72, 89, 90, 138. See also Mexicans in the United States.
Mexican American history, 139
Mexican anarchism, 101
Mexican authorities, 29; in Sonora, 32
Mexican Bajío, 7
Mexican consul: in Del Rio, Texas, 81; in Douglas, Arizona, 27, 32; in El Paso, Texas, 26, 40, 53, 55; in Los Angeles, California, 52; in Saint Louis, Missouri, 20, 79; in Tucson, Arizona, 48, 78
Mexican Federal Army, 42, 65
Mexican government, 45, 50, 59; agents of, 102
Mexican Independence Day, 23, 120
Mexican intellectual history, 139
"Mexican Joan of Arc," 81
Mexican laborers, 4, 48, 54, 59, 139
Mexican liberalism (Juárez liberalism), 3-4, 16, 21
Mexican nationalism, 2, 71
Mexican Revolution, 2, 6, 72, 112-114, 136-140
Mexican Supreme Court, 18
Mexicana, La (insurance company), 10
Mexicans in the United States, 120, 122, 139
Mexico, modernization of, 4
Mexico City, 50, 116
Mining, 4, 50
Minititlán, Veracruz, 25
Missouri (state), 52
Monitor Mexicano, El (Los Angeles, California), 36-37
Monitor Democrático (San Antonio, Texas) 64
Monterrey, Nuevo León, 5
Montjuich (Spain) fortress, 130-131
Morelos (state), 64
Morenci, Arizona, 21, 30-32, 48, 55, 72, 75, 78, 85, 103
Moret, Sam (Manuel Sarabia), 72
Mujer Moderna (San Antonio, Texas), 81-82
Muñoz Cota, José, 115
Murray, John, 84-85
Mutual Aid, 99

Nechayev, Sergei, 98
Neutrality Law violations, 48-49
New Mexico (state), 47, 50
New York City, 85
New York Times, 81, 87
Noveira, Rubén, 57
Norman, Lucía, 84
Nuevo León, 10, 19

Oaxaca (state), 1, 3, 16, 19, 50, 64, 101
Obregón, Alvaro, 139-140
Obrero, El, (San Antonio, Texas), 82
Obreros Libres, 30, 72
Ocampo, Guanajuato, 10
Oklahoma, 89, 122. See also Indian Territory.
Osollo, Luis, 11

Padua, Candido Donato, 64

Palomas, Chihuahua, 41-42, 44, 48, 50, 62, 65, 76-77, 81, 108, 127
"Palomas," 127, 163-167
"Pan American Labor League," 60, 83
Partido Liberal Mexicano (PLM), 10, 11, 14, 21, 24, 27, 29-30, 32-33, 38, 41-42, 47, 49, 52, 54, 62, 64, 72-73, 77, 79, 81, 93-94, 101, 104, 115-116, 121, 127; formation of, 15-19
"Passivity and Rebellion," 119
Pérez Escrich, 8
Philippines, 133
Phoenix, Arizona, 81
Pinkerton Detective Agencys, 88
Plan de La Noria, 3
Plaza Zaragoza (Monterrey, Nuevo León), 11
Political prisoners (United States), 85
Political Refugee Defense League (Chicago, Illinois), 85
Porfirian Mexico, 102. See also Díaz government and Porfiriato.
Porfiriato, 2-6, 21, 62, 84, 87, 101, 120, 127, 133.
Práxedis G. Guerrero: Artículos de Combate, 115, 134
Práxedis G. Guerrero: Artículos literarios y de combate; pensamientos; crónicas revolucionarias, etc., 114
presidente municipal (Janos, Chihuahua), 66
"Probable Intervention, The," 132
Programa y manifesto del PLM, 21, 23-24, 30, 72, 101
Progreso, El (San Antonio, Texas), 81
"propaganda by the deed," 98
Protestantism, 8, 9
Proudhoun, Pierre Joseph, 94-97, 99-100, 102
Puebla (state), 5, 10, 13, 50, 103
Puerto México, Veracruz, 25

Punto Rojo (El Paso, Texas), 54-55, 57-59, 62, 64, 82, 114-115, 119-122, 127, 135
"Puntos Rojos," 62, 83, 127, 134, 135
"Purpose of the Revolution, The," 109, 123, 143-145

racism and discrimination, 87, 89
radicalism, 103
railroad system (Mexican), 4, 5
Ramírez, José María G., 40
Ramírez, Sara Estela, 79
Ramírez Bonilla, 127
Rancho Colorado (Puebla), 11
Rangel, Jesús María, 42, 48, 53-54, 77, 108
Reform, The, 5, 6
Reforma, Libertad y Justicia (Austin, Texas), 42, 81
Reforma Social, La (El Paso, Texas), 24
Regeneración: published in Mexico City, 16-17; in San Antonio, Texas, 18; in St. Louis, Missouri, 18-19, 21, 23, 25, 27, 30; in Los Angeles, California, 61-62, 64, 66, 83, 85, 89-90, 112, 114-115, 122, 124, 127, 130, 134-135, 145, 147, 149, 153, 156, 163, 167
Regeneración, 1900-1918, 115
"Residents of El Paso," 120
Revolución (Los Angeles, California), 27-28, 32-35, 54, 73, 76, 84, 104, 108, 114-116, 118-119, 143
Revolt, of 1906, 101
"Revolutionary Episodes," 127, 163
"Revolutionary Women," 82, 134
Reyes, Bernardo, 10-11, 17, 103
Rhodakanaty, Plotino, 100
Rivera, Antonio, 64
Rivera, Concha, 62, 84, 87
Rivera, Librado, 16-17, 19, 25, 27-28, 33, 49, 52, 60-62, 64, 73, 76, 79, 81, 84,

101, 104, 114, 117
Rocksprings, Texas, 90-91, 134
Rodríguez, Antonio, 134
Rodríguez, Santana (Santanón), 64
Romero Rubio, Carmen (wife of Porfirio Díaz), 2, 5
Rousseau, Jean-Jacques, 8, 11, 94, 103
Rurales, 20, 27, 44, 65
Russia, 97-98, 103; Russian Revolution, 94, 98, 100

Sacco and Vanzetti Case, 130
Sacramento, California, 26
St. Louis, Missouri, 18, 21, 25, 49, 79, 81, 87, 101, 104
St. Louis (Missouri) newspapers, 79
St. Louis Post-Dispatch, 79
Salas, Hilario C., 25, 40
Salazar, José Inés, 38, 65
Saltillo, Coahuila, 41
San Antonio, Texas, 18, 33, 35, 42, 49, 53-55, 57, 60-61, 64, 75, 77, 79, 81, 87
San Antonio (Texas) newspapers, 82
San Felipe, Guanajuato, 7; newspaper in, 116
San Francisco, California, 13-14, 26, 48-49, 72, 77, 103, 116
San Juan de Ulúa (prison), 25, 27, 35, 41
San Luis Potosí, 9-11, 16-17, 19, 79, 101, 103
Sanftleben, Alfred G., 61
Sarabia, Juan, 16-19, 21, 24, 26-27, 30, 34, 39, 73-74, 78-79, 101; Guerrero as replacement for, 35; mother of, 87
Sarabia, Manuel, 17-19, 35, 42, 77-78, 81; as socialist, 102, 104, 112; influence on Guerrero, 30, 32, 72-76; kidnapping of, 27-28, 32-34, 87, 116,

120; marriage to Elizabeth Darling Trowbridge, 84-85
Sarabia (Labrada), Tomás, 33, 35, 42, 45, 53-54, 77-78, 81
Second Military Reserve, 10, 17, 78, 103
Secretaría de Educación Pública, 114-115
Siberia, 97
Silva, Benjamín, 40, 65
Silva, Prisciliano G., 24, 38, 40, 49, 65, 77-78; wife of, 88
Slavic peoples, 97
"Social Darwinists," 98
Socialists, American, 53
"Something Else," 62, 122
Sonora (state), 38, 64
Sonoran border cities, 23
South Texas, 39
Southern Europe, 97
Spain, 100; anarchism in, 99, 107; government, 130; immigrants, 100
Stevens, Charles F., 55
"Sweet Peace," 128
Switzerland, 97

Tabasco (state), 64
Taft, William Howard, 120
Tarrida de Mármol, Fernando, 32, 94, 100, 104
Terrazas (empire), 6, 64
Texas (state), 2, 27, 47, 50, 53, 55, 61, 77, 89, 108, 122, 138
textile mills, 4-6
tiendas de raya, 50, 60
"*Tierra y Libertad*" (slogan), 65
Tlachiquera, Guanajuato, 10
Tlaxcala (state), 5, 64
Tolstoy, Leo, 11, 94, 103, 109
Torreón, Coahuila, 41, 127
Toyah, Texas, 59

Treviño, Leocardio B., 40
Trowbridge, Elizabeth Darling, 73, 84-85
"True Interest of the Bourgeosie and the Proletariat, The," 110, 123, 145-147
Tucson, Arizona, 84
Turner, Ethel Duffy, 62, 65, 84-85
Turner, John Kenneth, 50, 59, 62, 64, 66, 84-85
Tuxtepec, Revolution (Plan) of, 1-3

Ulíbarri, Fidel, 35, 37
United States
United States Department of Justice, 26, 57-58, 60, 87-88
United States: government of, 59-60; agents of 102; attorneys, 73; consular agent, 58; informant, 82; marshals, 55, 85; other officials, 19, 29, 52; postal authorities, 20
United States intervention, 132-133
United States-Mexico borderlands, 72, 77, 89, 138
United States neutrality laws, 35, 88, 121
United States Secretary of State, 58

Vasconcelos, José, 114, 139
Vázquez, Manuel, 13, 30, 72
Velarde, Antonio, 57
Veracruz, 5, 25, 38, 40, 64
Verne, Jules, 8

"Victoria Segura," 82, 134
Viesca, Coahuila, 40-41, 61-62, 81, 104, 127
"Viesca," 127
"Vile Hatreds," 119
Villa, Pancho, 139-140
Villarreal, Antonio I., 18-19, 21, 24, 26, 28, 30, 33, 49, 52, 60-61, 73, 76, 78-79, 81, 84, 102, 104, 117
Villarreal, Próspero, 79, 87
Villarreal González, Andrea, 49, 79, 82, 87
Villarreal González, Teresa, 79, 82
Villarreal González sisters, 79, 82, 87, 134
Villarreal Márquez, Crescencio, 24
Vocación de Libertad, 115
Voz de la Mujer, La (El Paso, Texas), 82

Washington, D. C., 33
Washington Post, 44
Western Federation of Miners, 31-32
What is Property?, 95
"Whites, Whites," 90-91, 134, 141
"Whom Do You Love, Women?," 119
"Women," 134, 156, 158-163
Woodcock, George, 94
"Working," 111, 133, 153-156

Yucatán, 2, 127

Zamora, Emilio, 139